God's Saving Power
Studies in the Book of Romans

by
Gene Miller

Publication Board
of the Church of God
Warner Press
Anderson, Indiana

Many of the Bible quotations are the author's
own translation. Quotations from the Revised
Standard Version are copyright, 1952,
NCCCUSA, and are used by permission of the
copyright owners.

Contents

Chapter 1
The Letter to the Romans—What? Where? Who? Why?

Romans 1:1-15; 15:22-32

Objectives for Chapter 1:

1. To learn of the background and circumstances surrounding the writing of the Letter to the Romans.

2. To discover the apparent purposes for the writing of Romans.

3. To become familiar with some of the major themes and ideas which will be encountered in the study of Romans.

The Letter to the Romans, or Book of Romans, has long been widely accepted as the work of Paul the Apostle. In vocabulary, style, teachings, and subject matter it accords well with what we otherwise know about Paul. Specific internal evidence is strong; Paul is named as the author in the first verse of the letter, and numerous statements within it confirm Pauline authorship. It is the longest and most theologically comprehensive of all the

New Testament writing ascribed to Paul. Because of its approach to the great central themes of sin, condemnation or judgment, redemption or salvation, justification or right- eousness, faith, and hope, this book is consid- ered by many to be the most important doc- trinal writings of the New Testament. It is worthy of our closest attention and best efforts to understand.

As far as can be ascertained, the letter to the Romans was written while Paul was in Corinth, probably in A.D. 57 or 58. Though Paul had not yet visited the Christians at Rome (1:9-15), he had much wanted to do so, and was laying plans with that end in mind. He felt a keen sense of relationship and concern toward the church at Rome; he addressed them as "all God's beloved in Rome, who are called to be holy people." Furthermore, he spoke of how he thanked God for them in prayer, and asked that he might be able to pay them a visit.

We might well ask, "Why would Paul—or anyone—write such a letter or treatise to a group of people whom he had never visited or met?" (We will, however, see later in our study that Paul was apparently acquainted with sev- eral individuals in the Roman congregation.) He seems to have had several reasons for writing to the Roman church; these become apparent through careful study of the letter, particularly those passages given as background reading for this chapter. These reasons or purposes might be summed up as follows:

1. *To prepare the people for his proposed visit.* Paul speaks of how he wants to come to them so that he might "impart . . . some spiritual gift to strengthen" them (1:11) and receive encouragement and strength from them in return.

2. *To introduce to them his plan to go to Spain to preach the gospel, and enlist them in the effort.* Paul says that he hopes "to see you in passing as I go to Spain, and to be sped on my journey there by you" (15:24), literally, "to be sent on" or "sent forward." It is certain that Paul hoped for and expected the encouragement and spiritual backing of his readers; perhaps he also had in mind the possibility of their supporting his venture in material ways as well. He did go to Rome, of course, but as a prisoner, in chains. Some early tradition raises the possibility that Paul was released from his first imprisonment at Rome, preached the gospel "to the farthest limits of the west" (Spain?), and then was imprisoned again at Rome, where he met a martyr's death. At any rate, we know that the great apostle, preacher, and teacher did reach Rome, and that he maintained to the last his consuming ambition to proclaim the good news of Christ where Jesus' name had not yet been known or declared as Lord and Savior.

3. *Doctrinal or theological concerns.* While Paul does not state specifically that he writes for this

7

purpose, he obviously felt he needed to deal with serious Christian teachings in this communication. Furthermore, the questions to which he speaks in Romans are some of the most basic and vital in all Christian doctrine, and certainly would have been of primary concern in a city such as Rome—the question of sin, of the law, of idolatry and other pagan practices, of the place of the literal Jews and the Gentiles in God's plan, of salvation, of morality, and of justification or righteousness. Paul begins to write of these matters almost at the very beginning of the letter and continues until nearly the end.

The question of the literal Jews and the gospel is especially prominent in Romans; that clarification was certainly needed at Rome is evident from the Acts account of Paul's arrival and experiences there. (See Acts 28:17-28.) This account shows considerable resistance to the gospel on the part of the Jewish leaders in Rome. Paul may have also known, through reports which had reached him, of particular difficulties which existed at the Roman church, which was comprised of both Jewish and non-Jewish believers. So he used this letter as an occasion to speak to these problems. He must weld together these persons formerly alienated from each other by laws and traditions, now made one by faith in Christ. Romans 16:17-18 contains a pointed admonition regarding persons who "create dissensions and offenses, contrary to the doctrine which you learned." Paul may have known of such persons in the Roman congregation.

In the opening verses of his letter to the church at Rome, Paul introduces several of the themes and ideas which are prominent throughout the letter: the "gospel of God," Paul's apostleship to the Gentiles, his broader ministry and concern for "all men," faith, grace, peace, salvation, righteousness. As we read, study, and come to understand this great inspired writing, we will see these ideas appear again and again. Let each of them sink into your mind and heart as never before, and pray for the divine enlightenment of the Holy Spirit as you learn. You will want to keep in mind several key terms and their meanings in Romans as you study; here are some of the most significant:

Gospel—literally, good news or good tidings. In Romans, primarily the good news of redemption for all through faith in Christ.

Grace—the unmerited, unearned, undeserved favor or good will of God, particularly as it was and is manifested through Christ for salvation.

Peace—genuine inward wholeness and confidence, obtained through being related to the "God of peace" in Christ.

Righteousness (or *justification*)—the absolute uprightness and justness of God, and this same quality as it appears in human experience through faith. (More on this important concept later.)

Study and Review Questions for Chapter 1:

1. Why is Romans considered to be one of the most important doctrinal writings of all time?

2. List five key ideas or themes which will be involved in the study of Romans.

3. Describe briefly the circumstances surrounding the writing of Romans by Paul.

4. What are three apparent purposes or reasons for the writing of Romans?

Suggestions for Teaching

1. Stress the importance of each participant in the class or study group studying the appropriate biblical material, as well as the material in the text, beforehand. This will return rich dividends in the understanding of each part of Romans and in sustaining and increasing interest, fruitful class sessions, and personal benefit to the participant.

2. Strive to accomplish specifically the objectives given for each chapter, along with those which may be indicated by individual circumstances and needs or your own purposes in teaching the course. Reach the objectives first for yourself, and then help your pupils to do so.

3. Suggest that each person give careful attention to the study and review questions at the end of each chapter. This will serve as a tool

for establishing a thorough understanding of the material of that particular chapter and a test of self-comprehension.

4. Be sure to keep in mind the need for building the bridges of meaning and relevance between the situation in which and to which Romans was written and contemporary circumstances. (Example: Just as the gospel was given for and applied to Jews and Gentiles alike in the first century, so it is meaningful for all people, everywhere, in the twentieth century.)

5. If time permits, you may find it helpful to give brief tests or quizzes at several intervals during the quarter's study. This helps you to know how well you are leading the group into a thorough understanding of Romans, and it helps class members know how well they are assimilating the material. Such tests might include some of the questions at the end of chapters in the text, as well as others.

6. Both the teaching of these sessions and the understanding of what is taught will be facilitated and greatly increased in effectiveness if all participants use the same New Testament version or translation for biblical materials. The author recommends highly either the Revised Standard Version or the New American Standard Version.

Chapter 2
They Knew God, But—

Romans 1:16-2:11

Objectives for Chapter 2:

1. To learn the meaning of *righteousness* ("justi-fication, being justified") in Romans.

2. To discover the results of ignoring or rejecting God, and the fate of persons who so ignore or reject him.

3. To learn what Romans teaches about sexual immorality, particularly homosexuality.

4. To discover the promised rewards for those who are obedient to God and virtuous, and for those who are disobedient and evil.

In this section of Romans, Paul witnesses to his own regard for the good news of Christ, sent from God; he is "not ashamed" of it, because of what it *is* and what it *does*. This gospel, says Paul, is "the power of God for salvation." This salvation is "for everyone who believes"—both Jew and Greek, or Gentile. In this good news which affords salvation to those who believe, the "righteousness of God" is revealed. This term, *righteousness*, and particularly

the righteousness of God, is one of the most significant in Romans, and understanding it is vital to
understanding the book as a whole. *Righteousness,*
as employed by Paul in Romans, signifies especially "justness," freedom from partiality or
guilt, "vindication," or "justification," rather
than merely moral or ethical goodness, as it
often means in our common use. Hence, the
righteousness of God signifies primarily not the ethical personal character of God, but rather his
absolute justness, uprightness, and freedom
from partiality in all that he does. Persons can
find righteousness (be considered upright, justified, absolved of guilt for sin) only as they
receive it from God, through faith in Christ.
These ideas and metaphors have their roots in
Old Testament concepts and in legal processes
and judgments; Paul uses them very appropri-
ately in Romans, dealing with the position of
people before God and their relationship to the
law and to the good news of grace and salvation
through Christ.

Here, then, Paul declares that "God's kind of
righteousness," the kind of righteousness or
justification which is God's and which God
accepts, has been revealed and made possible
through the good news of Christ. This revelation has come "through faith for faith"; that is,
the justified standing with God must be under-
stood by faith and appropriated through faith.
In Romans 1:17, Paul reinforces this concept by

quoting from Habakkuk 2:4, which says, "Behold, he whose soul is not upright in him shall fail, but the righteous shall live by his faith."

Beginning with 1:18, Paul turns next to the other side of the issue. Just as surely as the righteousness of God is revealed in the gospel through faith, so "the wrath of God is revealed . . . against all ungodliness and wickedness. . . ." The remainder of chapter one is given to a description of the practices and the fate of those who are under the sentence of divine wrath or retribution. A God of true righteousness, justice, and impartiality cannot ignore the purposeful wickedness of evil persons any more than he can ignore the godliness and goodness of devout persons. Wrath and condemnation came upon these evil persons because they:

1. *Suppressed the truth.* This reminds one of Jesus' indictment against certain of his hearers, when He pronounced them doubly cursed because they not only refused themselves to enter the kingdom, but also hindered others who wished to enter.

2. *Had knowledge of God, but refused to acknowledge or serve him.* This aspect of Paul's description, represented in the title of this chapter, "They Knew God, But—" is perhaps the most severe indictment of those of whom he writes. They are "without excuse," for though God has revealed himself to them through his creation,

15

they refused to "honor him as God or give thanks to him." What a tragedy! And how common in every generation—including our own! Never has access to knowledge of God, to the good news of Christ, been so available to so many. At the same time, perhaps never have people so blatantly and widely and publicly flaunted their disregard for what they know, or could know, about God.

3. *Trusted in their own wisdom, and so became fools.* Such foolishness and misguided pride led them to one of the most prevalent evils and one of the most stubborn foes faced by the church in the early centuries—idolatry. How succinctly and masterfully Paul states the case as it really was and is! Such people, being fools and thinking themselves wise, had knowledge of an imperishable God, a God of glory. But they exchanged their relationship with this God for "a likeness of an image of perishable man and of birds and animals and snakes." Thus, they "exchanged the truth of God for the lie," and "worshiped and served the creature rather than the creator" (1:25).

4. *Knew God's condemnation upon sin, yet persisted in their sinful practices.* These evil persons knew not only that God was opposed to sin but also that he had decreed that "those who do such things are worthy of death" (1:32). Yet they continued to practice sin and to approve of others who did so. This is reminiscent of the words of the Lord

16

to Ezekiel: "But if you warn the wicked to turn
from his way, and he does not turn from his
way, he shall die in his iniquity" (Ezek. 33:9).
How many people do you know who practice
sin who do not know that God condemns sin?
Many will even acknowledge openly their
awareness of God's condemnation upon their
lives and the prospect of eternal death, but they
do not turn from their ways or from approving
of others in like practices.

The results of such attitudes, and the fate of
those who hold them and act accordingly, are
set forth graphically in this passage. First, they
"became futile in their thinking, and their senseless heart was darkened." History is replete
with evidence that whenever people turn
against God and trust in their own human "wisdom," they find themselves at the end of a
dead-end street. All striving after understanding and righteousness on human terms is futile.
When the light of the good news in Christ is
rejected, how great is the darkness in minds and
hearts! Jesus said, "If then the light in you is
darkness, how great is the darkness!" (Matt.
6:23).

Furthermore, Paul states, because of their
idolatry and their refusal to honor God, God
"gave them up [delivered them over] in the
lusts of their hearts to impurity" (1:24), and
"gave them up [delivered them over] to dishonorable passions" (1:26), and "gave them up

17

[delivered them over] to an unreprovable mind, to do things which are not acceptable" (1:28). Through his word, through the Spirit, through Christian evangels and friends, and in other ways God woos and pleads with such persons to renounce sin and acknowledge him. At the same time, he does not force his will or way on any individual. Persons who decide to reject God and the good news may do so; if they do, they will be subject to the consequences of their own decisions. God does not "give up on them," but he does allow them to go their own ways and to reap the appropriate harvests.

One of the most tragic and sordid aspects of the results of rejection, as delineated by Paul, is sexual immorality and perversion. In Romans 1:26-27, the sins of male homosexuality and lesbianism are specifically and pointedly condemned as "dishonorable," "unnatural," and "shameless." In a generation which is witnessing massive attempts to legitimize such practices, to make them "normal," and even to make them acceptable among Christians and in the church, this plain warning needs to be taught, preached, and published vigorously by all Christians. Such lusts and practices are grossly sinful in the sight of God. They issue from hearts and minds which are "darkened," "senseless," "impure," and in rebellion against God. It is notable that in these two verses, Paul does not employ the usual terms denoting "man" and "woman," but uses *arsenes* and *theleia*—"males" and "females," terms commonly employed to refer to male and female animals. Human experience has long born out what Paul makes plain—that such practices have serious consequences not only spiritually and eternally, but in the minds, hearts, and bodies of those who engage in them, "receiving in themselves the necessary penalty for their error [folly]."

Failure to acknowledge God led to even more extensive deterioration and sin; they became "filled with all kinds of wickedness." Read carefully, and then read again, the catalog of sins in Romans 1:29-31. Relationships are destroyed—with God, with family and friends, and with all people. Boldness in sin increases and influence widens—"sin loves company!" Many a young (and not so young!) person has been given a start down the way of sin by someone who, having become enmeshed and polluted and led astray, is more than willing to initiate another into that fellowship.

In the final part of this section of Romans (2:1-11), Paul begins to speak in the second person, turning the searchlight of judgment directly upon his readers. "Therefore, you are without excuse, O man, everyone who is judging. For when you judge the other man, you condemn yourself, because you who are judging are practicing the same things. Now we know that the judgment of God is according to truth upon those who practice such things." Paul points out that self-righteous condemnation of wrong in others does not gain the approval of God for oneself.

Verse 4 expresses a principle regarding the nature of God and his relationship to sin and sinful persons which every Christian ought to learn well: "Or do you presume upon the wealth of His kindness and forbearance and patience, not knowing that God's kindness leads you to repentance?" God's love for sinners, his forgiving mercy, his gift of a Son for sin, does not mean that God tolerates or condones sin. On the contrary, it indicates that God cannot tolerate sin, and that he has provided a way to escape its bondage and destruction. Far from approving sin or the sinner, God's tolerance is intended to give all people an opportunity to repent: "He is not willing that any should perish, but that all should come to repentance" (2 Pet. 3:9).

God's judgment comes into sharp focus in the closing verses of this section. His judgment will be "righteous," entirely just and true. It will be "to every man according to his deeds" (2:6), whether good or evil. To the evil, Paul promises "wrath," "fury," "tribulation," and "distress." To the good, he extends prospects of "eternal life," "glory and honor and peace." This judgment will fall upon "Jew and Greek alike, for with God there is no partiality" (2:10-11). This is the vital lesson which Peter learned at the home of Cornelius. In the Greek New Testament, the phrase translated "there is no partiality" is literally "there is no receiving of faces with God." In God's presence, at the judgment, "face" (outward appearance, personal pride, pretense, human glory) will be to no avail. God judges not according to "face," but "according to truth."

Study and Review Questions for Chapter 2:

1. What is the real meaning of the term *gospel* in Romans?

2. What is the usual meaning of the terms *righteousness* and *righteousness of God* in Romans?

3. List three reasons why God's wrath and condemnation were upon the persons of whom Paul wrote in this section of Romans.

4. List three specific results of rejecting God and trusting in one's own wisdom and passions, as set forth in this section of Romans.

5. How does God regard sexual immorality and perversion?

6. How will the final judgment show that "with God there is no partiality?"

Chapter 3
Will the Real Jews Please Stand Up?

Romans 2:12-3:31

Objectives for Chapter 3:

1. To learn the responsibility of the literal Jews under the new covenant.

2. To understand the penalty for hypocrisy.

3. To discover who are the "real Jews" in the gospel age.

4. To learn how God's righteousness is revealed through Christ and the new covenant.

5. To understand how all persons (both Jews and non-Jews) are on a common level before God and must find righteousness in the same way—by faith.

Having established that "there is no partiality with God," Paul proceeds to deal with a question which was prominent throughout the early years of the church, and no doubt was crucial at Rome. That question was, How does the concept of God's impartial judgment, including both Jew and non-Jew, bear upon the Jews

and their relationship to God through the law?
The answer is not easy or simple, but Paul
knows that it must be provided. Writing, we
believe, under the inspiration of the Holy Spirit,
he begins to develop his answer. As we will see,
one of the keys to this problem is to know who
the real or genuine "Jews" are *in terms of the new
covenant.*

First, Paul states, "Now as many as sinned
without law will also perish without law, and as
many as sinned in law will be judged by law."
This accords with the principle of God's righteous judgment—those who have been under law
will be held responsible for obedience to that
law. Thus, the "Gentiles" (literally, "the
nations"—that is, non-Jews) will be rewarded
for inner righteousness, for right actions, and
for clear consciences, even though they do not
have (the) law. God's judgment will be righteous and accurate, for he will judge the "secrets"
of people, not merely outward appearance or
actions.

In 2:17-24, Paul elaborates further on a
theme which he has already touched upon (2:1-
3). Here, the principle is applied particularly to
the Jews: If the Jews, with their knowledge of
the law, their positions as "teachers" and
"guides" and "correctors" of others, do the
things against which they teach, they will be
condemned just as others who do such things.
As did Jesus before him, Paul severely indicts

such hypocrisy, quoting the prophet Isaiah: "The name of God is blasphemed among the Gentiles (nations) because of you" (Isa. 52:5). Let this challenge strike home to *you* as a Christian. How often is God rejected, and the gospel made light of, among sinners because of self-righteous and hypocritical professors of Christ?

Moving toward the question of who the "real (genuine, true) Jews" are, in terms of the new covenant in Christ, Paul speaks next of circumcision. Although strictly physical in nature, circumcision played an extremely significant role in the old covenant between God and Israel; it was *the* mark of belonging to the God of Israel. Circumcision signified that a man was a possession of God and was dedicated to serving God alone. Here in Romans, Paul points out that this physical mark or rite has and retains such significance only as it issues in "keeping the law"— that is, in obedience to God by those who intended circumcision as a *sign* of the person's relationship to him, *not to bring about* that relationship. So then, "If the uncircumcised man keeps the precepts of the law, his uncircumcision will be considered as circumcision, will it not?" (2:27). Logically, then, the "real Jew" is not necessarily the one who has the outward mark of circumcision. Rather, the "real Jew" (that is, the person who really belongs to and serves God acceptably) is the person who has experienced the "real circumcision" as a "matter of the heart, spiritual and not literal" (2:29). Therefore, the "real Jews" (that is, the real chosen people of God) under the new covenant of grace are identified not by the physical mark of circumcision, but by a heart right with God and by the keeping of God's commandments. God still has a chosen people; he still has an "Israel," a nation of "Jews," but membership in this new family or nation of God is not through circumcision or natural ancestry. Rather, it is through faith, which produces righteousness.

Anticipating the next question which would come from a reader or debating opponent, Paul asks and answers it himself: "Then what advantage has the Jew? Or of what benefit is circumcision? Much in every way. Chiefly (or first), because they were entrusted with the words of God" (3:1-2). From this springboard, Paul establishes the following points:

1. Even though "some [of the Jews] were unfaithful" (did not fulfill the responsibilities as receivers and transmitters of God's oracles intended for all persons), this does not "nullify the faithfulness of God." In such circumstances, the righteousness and justness of God is vindicated and appears even more pronounced in comparison with the unfaithfulness of some persons.

2. The fact that God's faithfulness and righteousness is exhibited in sharp relief by human unfaithfulness does not justify either of two

false premises which are based upon a merely "human way" of thinking: (a) that God is unjust or unfair to "inflict retribution," since human unfaithfulness serves to highlight his faithfulness; (b) that persons ought to do evil so that God might be all the more glorified when his righteousness is observed in contrast to the evil deeds people do. At this point, Paul gives us an insight into one of the problems which he continually faced, and which is still often experienced by pastors, teachers, and other Christian leaders: "And why not, as we are blasphemed and as some claim that we say, 'Let us do evil so that good may come' " (3:8). Paul gives short shrift to such false reports and those who propagate them: "Their condemnation is just."

Though the Jews were privileged to be first "entrusted with the words of God," they have no advantage over Gentiles in terms of the new covenant. The reason for this, maintains Paul, is that "all men, both Jews and Greeks [non-Jews] are under sin." He fortifies this assertion by quoting from the psalms and from Proverbs, showing that universally people have gone astray and are out of harmony with God. These statements, from "the law" itself (the Old Testament) speak directly, Paul maintains, to those who are "in the law" (subject to the legal code). Thus, "all the world" becomes accountable to God, and all persons appear in need of salvation, for "no person will be justified (made righteous) before Him by works of law" (3:20).

This, then, leaves all persons in need of "the righteousness of God," or of "God's kind of righteousness." Such righteousness has been revealed, but is "apart from law." Indeed, it is "attested by the law and the prophets," but it comes only "through faith in Jesus Christ" and is for "all who believe." Under the new covenant in Christ, then there are not two ways of relating to God, one for Jews and another for non-Jews. Indeed, "there is no distinction, for all have sinned and fall short of the glory of God." Three important conclusions may be drawn about "justification" or "righteousness": (a) It comes "as a gift" and cannot be earned or worked for or deserved. (b) It comes by God's "grace," his unmerited favor. (c) It comes through "the redemption which is in Christ Jesus."

This justification through the sacrifice of Christ ("an expiation by his blood") demonstrates God's righteousness. In his mercy or forbearance, he "passes over the previously committed sins," and now, in the terms of the new covenant of faith in Christ, he shows his own righteousness as he justifies those who believe in his Son, fulfilling the terms of the covenant. The upshot of all this is that "the boasting is excluded" (3:27). Since all people have been declared to be "under sin," and since

no person can be justified by "works of law,"
then no one—Jew or Gentile—has any ground
for human "boasting." This exclusion comes not
through "a law of work," but through a "law of
faith," for "a man is justified [made righteous in
God's sight] by faith, apart from works of law"
(3:30). God is one; there is not one God for the
Jews and another for the Gentiles. Therefore,
this one God is God of both Jews and Gentiles.
He has chosen to justify, through Christ, all
persons on the principle of *faith*, "the circumcised by faith and the uncircumcised through
faith."

Paul was accused (and is still accused by
some) of being antinomian—an enemy of the
law. Realizing that what he has just said in this
section of Romans may well be interpreted as
being derogatory of the law, he hastens to point
out that the principle of justification by faith
does not "nullify" or "overthrow" the law.
Rather, it "upholds" or "establishes" the law,
since it is attested by the law and the prophets
and vindicates the righteousness of the God
who gave the law.

Study and Review Questions for Chapter 3:

1. What are some of Jesus' teachings about
hypocrisy which accord with Paul's statements
in Romans 2?

2. Who are the "real Jews," in term of the
new covenant in Christ?

29

3. What is meant by "circumcision of the heart?"

4. What advantages do Jews have over Gentiles in the new covenant?

5. How does the concept of "justification by faith" establish and fulfill the law?

Chapter 4
Abraham—The Faith and the Promise

Romans 4

Objectives for Chapter 4:

1. To learn what Abraham's personal relationship to God was and how he obtained and sustained that relationship.

2. To understand how a person cannot be justified before God by "works of law" but only by "faith."

3. To discover the meaning of spiritual ancestry and how God's promise to Abraham is fulfilled in this way.

Paul continues his consideration of justification, faith, works, and the law by turning to Abraham, the man who stood as spiritual and moral ancestor to the Jews. The author of Hebrews cites Abraham as an outstanding example of faith at work. Here in Romans Paul demonstrates that Abraham was justified (considered righteous before God) on account of that faith, rather than on account of what he

31

did. First, Paul points out that "if Abraham was justified by deeds, he has grounds for boasting, but not toward God" (4:2). In fact, as will shortly become evident, Abraham was *not* "justified by deeds." Even if he had been, he would have had no "ground for boasting" toward God, for his believing God (or faith in God) was what God counted to him as righteousness.

In the next five verses of this chapter, Paul contrasts the situation of one who works and receives due wages for labor, with one who does not work or attempt to win a reward but "believes in the one who justifies the ungodly." When one works, what one receives from the one served is not a "favor" but is what is owed. On the other hand, the one who does not trust in his or her own deeds but rather in a just and righteous benefactor has faith or trust which is "counted to him as righteousness." Again turning to the Old Testament, Paul quotes David (Psalm 32), expressing the blessing which rests upon those whose relationship to God is through divine forgiveness and justification.

If, then, the blessing and justification of God comes to those who are related to him through belief or faith, how does this bear upon the circumcised (literal Jews) and the uncircumcised (non-Jews)? In their insistence on circumcision (and other observances) according to the law even for Christians, the Jews disregarded the fact which Paul now brings to the attention of his readers: Abraham was counted as righteous before God through faith, and this took place *before* he was circumcised! Therefore, the example of Abraham himself, the literal and spiritual forefather of all the Jews, shows that circumcision does not provide or facilitate righteousness. On the contrary, Abraham received circumcision "as a sign, a certification [seal] of his righteousness through faith when he was uncircumcised" (4:11). Through this act of approval by God *before* circumcision, Abraham became the ancestor (spiritually speaking) of all who believe without circumcision, so that they are considered righteous because of faith, just as Abraham was. Now this might appear to limit Abraham's spiritual ancestry, and thus the imputation of justification or righteousness through faith, to Gentiles alone. Quickly, Paul makes it plain that this is not the case. Abraham is also the spiritual forefather of those who are circumcised, but who also follow Abraham's example in faith, thus being counted righteous or justified by faith, even as those who are not circumcised at all.

Now Paul has established firmly the principle that justification or right standing with God comes through faith, for both Jew and Gentile. The implications of this for Paul's readers and for us are far-reaching. One of the crucial questions which it raises is simply this: If, as Paul maintains, the good news of redemption in

Christ is equally for all persons, if there is no advantage in being a literal Jew, if outward circumcision or works of law are no longer important in the spiritual scheme of things, then what about the *promise?* The promise of "inheriting the world" was made to Abraham and to his descendants. The literal Jews are his descendants, the family of Abraham. How then could others (non-Jews) have a share in this inheritance?

Paul apparently anticipates the question and answers it directly. The promise to Abraham and his posterity did not come "through law" or human descent, but "through the righteousness of faith." The fulfillment of the promise, then, is not to the "adherents of the law," but to all those who "share the faith of Abraham." Thus, all (both the literal Jews and the Gentiles) who are related to God by faith are heirs of the promise. Under this condition, the fulfillment of the promise rests entirely upon the grace and favor of God, and can be made available to all who believe in Christ as Lord and Savior.

In verses 17-21, Paul gives an inspiring and insightful description of the kind of faith which Abraham exercised. He believed in a God "who gives life to the dead and calls the things which do not exist as existing" (v. 17). Trusting in this kind of God, Abraham believed against all outward indications and circumstances that God's promise would be fulfilled, and that he would become "the father of many nations." He was "fully convinced that God was able to do what he had promised" (v. 21). No wonder Abraham's faith was "counted to him as righteousness!" What about your faith? What about the faith of other Christians whom you know? Does your faith persist even in the face of discouragement, obstacles, seeming impossibilities? Abraham "was empowered by faith, giving glory to God." Does your faith cause you to believe in God's promises without wavering or uncertainty, no matter what the circumstances?

This heritage of faith from Abraham has belonged to Old Testament Israel, to the prophets, to the apostles—but this is not all. Even now, and as long as the world stands, righteousness (justification) based upon faith is and will be counted to all who have Abraham's kind of faith. For us, however, a vital new element has come into the picture. Abraham believed in God, in God's word, and in God's promises. We, of course, must also believe in God in the same way. But our faith, the faith which will be "counted to us as righteousness," is in a God who not only created the universe, brings the dead to life, and keeps his promises, but who also "raised from the dead Jesus our Lord." Furthermore, this faith includes belief in this Jesus as the one who "was delivered up because of our trespasses and was raised for our justification." Just as Abraham's faith and the promise to Abraham were prior to and independent of the law, and Abraham's justification came by faith, the same is true under the new covenant. As "spiritual descendants" of Abraham, those who find favor with God must be justified before him on the basis of faith, faith in the death of Christ for the forgiveness of their sins, and his resurrection for their victory over sin and death.

Study and Review Questions for Chapter 4:

1. Why was Abraham a good choice for Paul to employ as an example of faith?

2. Why was Abraham's faith "counted to him as righteousness" or justification in God's sight?

3. How did Paul show that Abraham's standing with God did not depend on circumcision or on "works of law?"

4. Explain how God has been true to his promise to "Abraham and his posterity" even though the covenant and justification have been extended to all, Jew and Gentile alike.

5. How is saving Christian faith like the faith of Abraham? How is it different?

6. Upon what is the unity of Jewish and non-Jewish believers to be based?

Chapter 5
Justified by Faith—for Peace, Life, Righteousness

Romans 5

Objectives for Chapter 5:

1. To learn how justification by faith brings peace, life, and hope to the believer.

2. To consider how we can be reconciled to God through Christ.

3. To learn how Adam typifies sin, and therefore death, in human experience, and how Christ brings righteousness and life.

"**S**o then, having been justified by faith, let us have peace with God through our Lord Jesus Christ" (5:1). As Paul begins to consider the results of justification (being made righteous) by faith it is significant that he speaks first of "peace." In our study of Romans 7 and 8, we will see that Paul knew only too well the strife and "warring" which plagues those who are not "in Christ," but are attempting to relate to God through law or deeds. Furthermore, Paul viewed his own ministry and the Christian message in general as one of "reconciliation." Through Christ real peace can come to a person's life; this peace can be experienced only by those who have been "justified by faith." In his exhortation to "let us have peace with God," Paul employs the present subjunctive, signifying a continuing relationship and standing: "Let us be having and continue to have peace with God."

Having peace with God, one can also "rejoice." Truly, real peace leads to joy! Through Christ, Paul points out, we are able to stand in God's grace and "rejoice in hope of the glory of God." What a great hope we as Christians have that we will someday share in God's own glory! Peter says, "and when the chief Shepherd is revealed you will obtain the unfading crown of glory" (1 Pet. 5:4). Paul speaks in 1 Thessalonians 2:12 of "God, who calls you into his own kingdom and glory."

But the rejoicing of those who are "justified by faith" is not limited to their anticipation of the glory of God. On the contrary, they rejoice even "in hardships" (tribulations). How can this be? Study carefully the "ladder of experience" which Paul builds upon this concept in verses 3-5: Christians rejoice even in the midst of hardships—because hardships produce endurance; and endurance produces character; and character produces hope; and this hope does not disappoint those who possess it; because it is sustained and supported by the love of God, which "has been poured into [their] hearts through the Holy Spirit. . . ."

Does this describe your experience as a Christian? Does it describe the experience of other Christians whom you know and observe? Do you "rejoice" in the midst of hardships or tribulation in serving God, or do you become discouraged and downhearted? Does hardship develop your endurance and steadfastness, or does it weaken you spiritually? When you endure or undergo trials, does your character stand the test and grow even stronger and more resolute, or do your faith and courage begin to fail? Does your hope in God grow even stronger, along with the knowledge that you will not be disappointed in this hope, because it is assured by God's love through the Spirit?

Justification by faith brings not only peace, joy, and hope but also deliverance or freedom. As Paul well knew, people alone could not free themselves from bondage to sin; we were "helpless" or "weak" in our predicament. God knew this, and "at the right time" sent Christ to "die for the ungodly." In human relationships, it is rare for a person to lay down his or her life for another—even for a "righteous man." By contrast God, being a God of mercy, grace, and love, demonstrated that love to all persons for all time by sending his Son to die for those who were "yet sinners." It follows that such a great sacrifice on God's part, consisting of the very blood of Christ, not only justifies those who believe, but also "saves them from wrath." (Paul refers here to the "wrath" which has been "revealed from heaven against all ungodliness and wickedness," and which will come at the day of "God's righteous judgment." See Romans 1:18, 2:5.)

Through Christ's death for sin, then, we are "reconciled" to God and justified in his sight. Furthermore, we are assured of eternal salvation and life through our Savior's triumph over death and the grave. This means that we can experience freedom from sin, and thus new life. Employing the contrasting pairs "sin and death" and "righteousness and life," Paul builds the following analogy (5:19):

Sin came into human experience through one man—Adam.	Justification came into human experience through one—Christ.
Death followed sin.	Life follows justification.
Death spread to all persons because everyone sinned.	Life is made possible for all people through the "free gift" of God.

Bringing the analogy to a close, Paul points out that just as Adam's trespass initiated sin into human experience and resulted in the death of many, so the gift of God's grace, mediated through the sacrifice of Christ, results in life for many. The judgment following trespass or sin could be only condemnation, and so it was; but the sentence was lifted by Christ, the "free gift following many trespasses" which brings justification. In yet further comparison, Paul expresses the situation in these terms:

One man's trespass	led to	Condemnation for all.
One man's act of righteousness	led to	Righteousness and life (justification).
One man's disobedience	led to	Many being constituted sinners.
By one man's obedience	led to	Many shall be constituted righteous.

At the close of this chapter, Paul returns briefly to the function of the law in the total scope of God's dealing with mankind. "Now law came in alongside, so that the trespass was increased. But where sin increased, grace increased exceedingly more, so that just as sin reigned by death, so also grace might reign through righteousness for eternal life, through Jesus Christ our Lord" (5:20-21). Here, Paul expresses an idea about which he will have more to say later—that when law came, trespasses or sins appeared even more prevalent and more sinful, as they were seen in the light of the commandment of a holy God. Thus, the law served to show sin as it really was and to awaken the realization of condemnation for sin. At the same time, law could not fully deliver from that condemnation; only "grace," the free gift or favor of God, could do this, establish righteousness, and lead to eternal life.

Study and Review Questions for Chapter 5:

1. What is the significance of "peace with God" or "reconciliation" in Romans 5? What part does this idea play, or ought it to play, in Christian experience? in Christian witness and ministry?

2. How can hardship (trial, tribulation) produce endurance or steadfastness in Christian living?

3. Explain the particular function of Christ's death and his continuing life in Christian experience, as expressed in Romans 5.

4. In what way was Adam a "type" (or "antitype") of Christ?

5. Does Paul say in Romans 5 that God gave the law so that sin would increase? Explain your answer.

Chapter 6
What about Sin?
Romans 6:1-8:2

Objectives for Chapter 6:

1. To learn where Christians stand in relation to sin and its power, and how they can have victory over sin.

2. To discover the true significance of Christian baptism.

3. To understand and accept the assurance that because Christ conquered death and now lives, those who believe in him shall do likewise.

4. To learn what Christians are free from, and to what and whom they are enslaved, in Christ.

5. To understand the relationship of Christians to the law.

6. To see how sin, working through the flesh, enslaves; and correspondingly, how Christ, through the Spirit, frees from sin and death.

Paul, at this point, turns to a question which was of burning importance to all Christians of his day and of every generation, including our own. The question is of sin's relation to the believer's life and experience. The apostle has already denied emphatically the conclusion which some had reached, and even attributed to him, that we should "do evil so that good may come" (Romans 3:8). Here at the beginning of chapter 6 he refutes a related concept: "Shall we continue in sin, so that grace may increase?" His answer is an emphatic phrase which he often employed to express especially strong denial or disapproval—literally, "let it not be!" In contemporary English, a good rendering is "by no means!" or "certainly not!" It is unthinkable that the person who has been redeemed from sin by the blood of Christ should continue to live in sin! Let us follow Paul carefully as he develops this vital theme.

First, Christians cannot continue to live in sin, because they "have died to sin." At this point, the true significance of Christian baptism comes clearly into focus. All who have been "baptized into Christ Jesus" (that is, who have received Christian baptism, been immersed in the name of Christ) have been "baptized into his death." Therefore, symbolically, these persons share in the death and resurrection of Jesus Christ. In the act of baptism the believer is "buried" under the water, as Christ was buried in the earth, which speaks of his dying to self, sin, and the world. In like manner, the believer is "raised" as Christ was raised from death "through the glory of the father." After this spiritual "death" and "resurrection" the believer can "walk [live] in newness of life" (6:4).

Only after Christ willingly experienced death could he experience the resurrection. So it is with believers in their "death" to sin and "resurrection" to new life: "for since we have become united in the likeness of his death, we shall certainly also be united in the likeness of his resurrection." This is made possible because "our old man [self] was crucified with him" It is through the "old man" or "old self" and through "the flesh" that sin operates. Therefore, as long as this "old man" lives and exercises control in one's life, that individual will be under the dominion of sin. This old self, in genuine Christian experience, is "crucified" as the body of Christ was crucified or put to death. Thus, one is no longer "enslaved to sin." In fact, Paul goes on to assert that the person who has "died" (to sin) has been "acquitted of sin" (justified, declared not guilty of sin).

Deliverance from enslavement to sin, however, is only one side of the issue. "Since we died with Christ, we believe that we shall also live with him" (6:8). Christ was raised from the dead once only and once for all, after dying once only and once for all. Having experienced this, he "will never die again," because "death no longer rules over him." Jesus, when he died, died "to sin" and now "lives to God." So it is with the redeemed person; we have "died to sin" once and for all, and have now come "alive to God in Christ Jesus." This resurrection, like its preceding death, is not the resurrection "at the last day" of which Martha spoke to Jesus. Rather, it is the resurrection of *today*—experienced by every true believer! So Jesus replied to Martha, "I am the resurrection and the life. He who believes in me, even if he dies, he shall live; and everyone who is living and believing in me shall never die" (John 11:25-26). New life begins *now*, eternal life begins *now*—for the one who is willing to die to self and sin and come alive to live a new life for God in Christ.

Now since Christ triumphed over sin through his death and resurrection, this same victory is available to those who believe in him and who share in "the likeness of his death" and the "likeness of his resurrection." Since this is true, exhorts Paul, "Do not let sin reign in your mortal bodies, to cause you to obey its lusts" (6:12). This admonition is in the imperative mood—"Don't do it!" As morally responsible beings, Christians must choose and keep on choosing not to allow sin to gain any mastery in their lives. Furthermore, specifically, they must not allow their "members" to be used as "instruments of unrighteousness" by sin. Rather, they must each present themselves "to God as a living person from the dead," and yield their "members as instruments of righteousness to

God." This is made possible by the glorious fact that sin no longer has lordship over such persons, for they are "not under law but under grace."

Does being "under grace" and not "under law" give one license? Does freedom from bondage to sin make one "absolutely free?" Again, Paul says emphatically, "Certainly not!" The concept of being "under sin," "under grace," and "under the law" signifies in Romans *subjection to* these powers or influences. Therefore, persons who are unredeemed—"under sin"—are in subjection to sin. They sin not only because they wish to do so (often the opposite is true), but they are "obedient" to sin and do its bidding, because they are enslaved to it. By the same token, persons who are "in Christ" have been freed from subjection to sin, and so they no longer obey its dictates. At the same time, however, they become subject to another "bondage"; they are "slaves of righteousness." This is a great and glorious truth; Paul says, "Thanks be to God that you who once were slaves of sin became obedient from the heart to the standard of teaching to which you were delivered!" (6:17). Formerly, these persons had presented their members "to impurity and to lawlessness upon lawlessness," but now they are directed to present them "to righteousness for holiness."

Paul next calls upon his readers to draw upon their own personal experience; let each of us do likewise as we think about the last few verses of Romans 6. When you were a "slave of sin," what results did you have then "of which you are now ashamed?" Or, if even now you are a slave of sin, what kind of harvest are you reaping and what kind do you expect to reap, from your present life and conduct? No matter what sin may promise, it can deliver, finally, only one "wage" or "reward"—death. "For the end [finish, consummation] of these things is death" (6:23). James says, "Then desire when it has conceived gives birth to sin; and when sin is full-grown it brings forth death" (James 1:15).

So "the wages of sin is death," but thanks to God, there is another way! When Christ has set one free from sin's bondage, that one becomes a "slave of God" (or, as Paul puts it on another occasion, a "fool for Christ"). While the result of sin and its accompanying deeds is death, the result of becoming a "slave of God" is "fruit for holiness, and the end [consummation] eternal life." This whole chapter is summed up admirably in verse 23: "For the wages of sin is death, but the free gift [grace-gift] of God is eternal life in Christ Jesus our Lord."

7:1-6

Having established that the redeemed person is freed from the bondage of sin, Paul takes up in detail a kindred question: What about the Christian (both Jewish and Gentile) and the law? His first statement reminds his readers of a commonly known principle of the law: "The law rules over a person as long as he lives" (7:1). Citing a specific example from common life, Paul says: "So the married woman is bound by law to the living husband. But if the husband dies, she is released from the law of the husband." Under these provisions in the law at that time, a woman would be "considered an adulteress" if she became the wife of a different man while the husband was living. By the same token, if the husband died, and the woman was "free from the law of the husband" as the law provided, then she would not be considered an adulteress if she became the wife of another man.

Passing immediately to the point which he wishes to make through this analogy, Paul reminds his readers: "Just so, my brothers, you also were caused to die to the law, through the body of Christ, so that you might belong to another—to the one who has been raised from the dead—so that we might produce fruit for God" (7:4). The redeemed person, then, is like the woman whose husband has died. Just as she is no longer bound to him but is free to belong to another, so the Christian has been freed from the law in order to belong to a new Master—Christ.

Notice that there is a purpose for this new freedom and life, gained "through the body of Christ": "that we may produce fruit [produce results] for God." Echoing the thought of 6:23, the apostle points out again that those who are "living in the flesh" are subject to the passions of sins" and are "producing fruit for death." On the other hand, those who by dying to the law have been freed from it serve God "in newness of spirit and not in oldness of letter." Faith in Christ releases us from bondage to a written legal code and replaces such a code by spiritual renewal, and we become new persons. This "renewal of spirit" comes through the Spirit: "The letter kills, but the Spirit gives life" (2 Cor. 3:6). Jesus himself said, "It is the Spirit that gives life, the flesh is of no avail" (John 6:63).

7:7—8:2

In the light of this, then, what is the relationship of "the law" to "sin?" One aspect of this question has already been dealt with in Romans 5, but more must be said. The person who is "under law" is also described as "living in the flesh," subject to "the passions of sins which through the law operate in our members to produce fruit for death." So there is a relationship, indeed, a close association, between "the law" and "sin." Paul recognizes this relationship, in part through his own personal experience; but he does not consider these two forces or influences to be identical in any sense. Furthermore, he wants to make sure that his readers do not so identify or understand them. In 7:7-

12, the following basic premises appear:

1. The law is not sin, nor is it sinful. On the contrary, it is "holy and just and good."

2. The law, by setting forth definite standards, brought awareness of sin, such as covetousness.

3. Sin took advantage of a person "through the commandment" and accomplished in that person "all kinds of covetousness."

4. Sin was not able to exert its power fully until the commandment came, since the person was not aware of the righteous and just standards of the law, and so had no realization of transgression.

5. When the commandment did come, (when the person became aware of and responsible to the law) sin "came to life" and the person "died" because he or she was found to be in violation of the law.

6. Note especially this factor—when sin had "taken opportunity through the law," it "deceived" and "killed" the person. This is one of the basics of the operation of sin and the devil, the prince of sin. The term *devil* (from Greek *diabolos*) means "a deceiver." Sin, stemming from the master deceiver, took advantage of the realization of sin which came through the law and, by deception, brought spiritual death to its victim. Thus, the commandment which was intended to lead to life through faithful obedience resulted instead in death.

51

In this entire section, 7:7—8:2, Paul employs the first person singular in explicating the relationship between the law and sin. Certainly this was appropriate, first because Paul himself had experienced what he describes. Second, the description is universally applicable and reveals the state of all people before and after they meet Christ. Before salvation, all are "under law"—if not under Jewish law, under the "law of sin and death." Before salvation, all are "in the flesh," all are influenced by "the passions of sins," all are "producing fruit for death," all are plagued by knowledge of what is right but are unable to do the right.

We may be sure that in this "first person" section, Paul begins by speaking of his life before Christ (7:7-25, with the exception of the parenthetical expression "Thanks be to God through Jesus Christ our Lord!" in 25a) and then of his life and experience after Christ (8:1-2). If you are not a Christian, see your own predicament mirrored in the inspired word, and accept deliverance from the "law of sin and death!"

In 7:13, Paul reinforces his former assertion that the law as such did not "become death" for him. Rather, "It was sin, that it might appear as sin, accomplishing death for me through what was good." Thus, sin was shown to be "exceedingly sinful," exposed in its true nature when viewed in the light of the commandment, which was good. In 7:14-25, Paul not only employs the first person singular, but also the present tense. This does not indicate that these conditions existed at the time when Paul wrote the words. It does serve to emphasize the reality of the experience and its relevance for all persons. Such use of the present tense is common in the Gospels and throughout the Greek New Testament.

First, Paul acknowledges that while "the law is spiritual," he himself is "fleshly, having been sold under sin." Furthermore, he finds himself in a puzzling and discouraging dilemma: "I do not know what I am accomplishing." (Or, in English vernacular, "Sometimes I don't know what I'm doing.") His total situation he describes as follows:

What I do not wish to do, this I practice; and what I hate, this I do.

Since I do not wish to do what I do (because I know it is wrong), I agree with the law, that it is good (since the law forbids such practices);

therefore, since I am practicing these things against my own will or desire,

it is not really I myself who am doing these things, but the sin which dwells in me.

This is not simply "passing the buck" to avoid responsibility, nor is it "theological shenanigans" for the sake of avoiding an issue, nor does it furnish grounds for continuing in sin. Paul gives here a brutally honest analysis of the human predicament outside Christ.

The apostle finds, then, that there is another "law" in addition to the law to which he has been previously referring. This other law is the law which decrees, "When I wish to do the good, the evil lies close at hand." This law is in opposition to God's law, so that even though Paul says, "In the inner person I delight in the law of God," and "I myself serve the law of God with my mind," yet he must also say, "I am captive to the law of sin which dwells in my members, and with the flesh I serve the law of sin." Crying out in passionate exclamation as he often does, Paul expresses the despair of this dilemma and then anticipates the victorious conclusion which is about to be developed: "I am a wretched man! Who shall deliver me from the body of this death? Thanks be to God through Jesus Christ our Lord!"

The term *therefore* at the beginning of Romans 8 is of great significance; it indicates that what follows it is based upon and closely connected with what has gone before. Since there *is* deliverance from the "law of sin and death," and that deliverance is through Jesus Christ our Lord, there is "no condemnation for those who are in Christ Jesus." This "law" has been unseated by another higher and more powerful "law"—the "law of the Spirit of life in Christ Jesus." The dilemma which is created by sin, working through the weakness of "the flesh" and the demands of the law, has been overcome. Certainly we can join with Paul in crying out, "Thanks be to God!"

Study and Review Questions for Chapter 6:

1. According to Paul in Romans 6, why is it unthinkable that the redeemed person should continue to live in sin?

2. Explain the significance and symbolism of Christian baptism, according to Romans 6.

3. What does it mean to be "under law" and "under grace?"

4. What are the immediate and the ultimate results of sin and of salvation, respectively?

5. How can one be delivered from the "law of sin and death?"

Chapter 7
The Spirit Conquers

Romans 8:3-39

Objectives for Chapter 7:

1. To learn what it means to "live according to the flesh" and "according to the Spirit."

2. To learn the results of "having one's mind set on the flesh" and "having one's mind set on the Spirit."

3. To understand the Christian's relationship as a "child of God," "an heir of God," and a "fellow heir with Christ."

4. To learn how the Spirit works with Christians in intercession and prayer.

5. To see God's total plan for his people in Christ—foreknowledge, pre-planning, calling, justification, glorification.

6. To learn why and how Christians are "more than conquerors" through Christ.

The victory over the "law of sin and death" is made possible by God's gift of his Son, who came "in the likeness of sinful flesh and concerning sin," and thus he "condemned sin in the flesh" (8:3). Here is one of the truly marvelous aspects of Christian redemption! The divine Son of God took upon himself the very nature or bodily form through which sin had been wielding its power and deception. As a man, he overcame and thus "condemned" sin in the very sphere in which it held sway. As a result, the "righteous requirement of the law" *could* be fulfilled in the hearts and lives of individuals—not by further or more strenuous human effort or will, but in "those who walk [live] not according to the flesh but according to the Spirit" (8:4).

This thought introduces two important concepts which form the basis of the section 8:5-17: "To walk according to the flesh [Spirit]" and to "set one's mind on the things of the flesh [Spirit]." The lines are sharp and clear, and the meanings go to the heart of each person's manner of life and inner orientation. While some persons conduct themselves according to the dictates of the passions and desires of sin and the flesh, others conduct themselves according to the directions of the Spirit within. Likewise, some have their thoughts and concerns centered on self and the desires of the flesh, while others have their thoughts centered on spiritual objectives and values. Which of these describes you, your life, and your interests? In this passage, Paul employs the term *flesh* (Greek *sarx*) not in the sense of the physical body alone, but with reference to the "old man," or selfish, unregenerated nature which is in opposition to God and to the Spirit.

Notice carefully the comparison between these two opposites:

In the flesh	*In the Spirit*
Living according to the flesh	*Living according to the Spirit*
Thinking about things of the flesh	*Thinking about things of the Spirit*
Death	*Life and peace*

These two kinds of being and living are naturally and mutually exclusive, and "never the twain shall meet." In his letter to the Galatian Christians, Paul said: "For the flesh desires what is contrary to the Spirit, and the Spirit desires what is contrary to the flesh. These two lie in opposition to one another, so that you might not do what you want" (Gal. 5:17). Here in Romans 8:7-8 this principle is explained and reinforced: "The mind set on the flesh is in enmity toward God, for it is not in subjection to the law of God, nor is it able to be." Since this is the case, those who are "in the flesh" [that is thinking about the things of the flesh and living according to its desires] cannot please God." A sobering thought, indeed! If you are "in the flesh" in this sense, you may have the best of intentions, you may want to do right ever so much, you may struggle to please God—all to no avail! Only by accepting the Son of God, who has already defeated sin in the flesh, the area of its operation, can you find the way to "life and peace."

In 8:9-17, Paul turns again to second person, addressing his readers concerning their own spiritual state as believers, and considering what this relationship entails. The test is the presence and guidance of the indwelling Spirit. "Now you are not in the flesh but in the Spirit, if in fact the Spirit of Christ dwells in you. But if anyone does not have the Spirit of Christ, this person does not belong to Him" (8:9). This is reminiscent of 1 John 3:24: "By this we know that he remains in us, by the Spirit which he gave to us." Do you know that you belong to Christ, because you feel and acknowledge the inner witness of the Spirit? If the Spirit dwells within, so then does Christ. If Christ and his Spirit dwell within, believers may be sure also that:

1. Their fleshly (bodily) passions have been "put to death" and they have "come alive" spiritually.

2. They will be sustained, both physically and spiritually, by that divine life of Christ dwelling within.

3. They are no longer "debtors" (under obligation or bondage) to live "according to the flesh."

4. Each is a true son or daughter of God, for "as many as are led by the Spirit of God, these are the sons of God."

As a son or daughter, one does not receive, says Paul, a "spirit of slavery for fear," but a "spirit of sonship, by which we cry out, 'God, [our] father!'" Furthermore, "the Spirit himself witnesses with our spirit that we are children of God." Being assured of such a Father-child relationship, Christians can also confidently expect an inheritance from their heavenly Father; in addition, they become "fellow heirs" with their "elder brother" in God's family—Jesus Christ himself! This inheritance cannot be eroded away or destroyed or diminished in any way, for it is "an inheritance which is imperishable, undefiled, and unfading, kept in heaven for you" (1 Pet. 1:4).

There is, however, a condition—not a catch, but a condition—plainly noted by Paul in Romans 8:17: "if in fact we suffer with him, so that we may also be glorified with him." Are we willing to meet the condition, to be willing really to suffer with (feel along with, share in real compassion with) Christ, so that we, even as he was, may in turn be "glorified" with him? Paul hastens to add to this challenge his conviction that "the sufferings of the present time are not worthy of comparison with the glory which will be revealed in us" (8:18). Indeed, so great is this glory that even the "creation" awaits expectantly (literally, "with head stretched forward") the "revealing of the sons of God." Even the created universe was "subjected to futility," but

that subjection was "in hope." This hope will be
fulfilled, because "even the creation itself shall
be set free from the bondage of decay [corrup-
tion] into the freedom of the glory of the children of God" (8:21). Both "all the creation" and
"we ourselves," says Paul, have been "groaning
and travailing," awaiting the day of redemption.
Here in verse 23, Paul speaks of the final act or
consummation of God's work in his people—
"sonship, the redemption of our bodies." We
already have the "first produce" or "first results"
of God's redemptive act in the person of the
indwelling Spirit, but we still must wait for
"sonship [that is, the full realization of our son-
ship], the redemption of our bodies."

Living in anticipation of their inheritance, of
their final resurrection and the final revelation
of God's glory in and through them, God's people are sustained by two great forces or supports—"hope," in which they were saved in the
first place, and "the Spirit," who "takes hold
with us in our weakness." How often it is true
that "we do not know how to pray as we
ought!" Here, Paul gives assurance that the
Spirit "intercedes in our behalf" (8:26), expressing what we cannot express in words. God,
who "searches the hearts of all men," knows
also the intention and thought of the Spirit,
when the Spirit intercedes for the holy people.

Romans 8:28 has been much mistranslated
and as a result, much misinterpreted. Let us

note carefully what it says: "Now we know that with those who love God, he works all things for good, with those who are called according to [his] purpose." God accomplishes this work specifically as follows:

Those whom he *knew beforehand*,
he also *planned beforehand* that they be conformed to the image of his Son;
those for whom he planned beforehand,
he also *called*.
those whom he called,
he also *justified*;
and those whom he justified, he also *glorified*.

God, in his divine wisdom, knew beforehand that some would accept his call. Knowing this, he planned beforehand that they would become like Christ, his Son; "A disciple . . . when he is fully taught, will be like his Master" (Luke 6:40). Having known and planned beforehand regarding these persons, he called them. (God's call goes out to all; here, as often in the New Testament, *called* means "called and was heard and accepted.") Having called them [to repentance and faith in Christ], he justified them [made them righteous] through that faith. To those who have been thus foreknown, foreplanned, called, and justified, God promises that they will be "glorified"—they will "share in his own glory" (8:29-30).

This section closes with one of the most triumphant passages in the entire New

Testament—8:37-39. It has given encouragement, comfort, strength, and new determination to thousands of God's people over the centuries. Read it carefully, and let it sink into your
mind and heart as never before. Notice how
Paul builds up the basis of Christian assurance,
hope, and triumph block by block, and crowns
the structure with some glorious affirmations:

God is for us; He gave his own Son for us.

God is the one who justifies us (judges us
righteous).

Christ Jesus was raised from the dead; he
stands even now at the Father's right hand;
he intercedes for us.

THEREFORE:

Who can stand against us? No one!

God will give us all things—in addition to his
Son!

When God justifies, no one can condemn.

Like Christ, we shall be raised from the dead.
Christ is alive, with God the father in
heaven.

We need not trust in ourselves or in human
or worldly powers.

Nothing shall separate us from the love of
Christ!

In short, "we are surpassingly victorious
through the one who has loved us!" Not just
conquerors; more than conquerors! Not merely
overcoming, but overcoming with flying colors
all foes, opponents, and threats! How glorious

to be thus kept in "the love of God in Christ Jesus our Lord!"

Study and Review Questions for Chapter 7:

1. Explain how God did what the law could not do, with regard to the problem of sin.

2. What does it mean to "live according to the flesh" and "to live according to the Spirit?"

3. What is the test of true relationship to Christ (8:9)?

4. What is the condition for receiving an inheritance under God?

5. In what sense are Christians still waiting for the consummation of their salvation?

6. How do Christians know that they are, or can be, "surpassingly victorious" or "more than conquerors?"

Chapter 8
The Gospel and the Israelites

Romans 9:1-11:36

Objectives for Chapter 8:

1. To feel Paul's deep concern for his fellow Jews.

2. To understand Paul's explanation of how God's promises and covenants have been fulfilled, not through law and human ancestry but through faith and God's own sovereign election, mercy, and grace.

3. To see why and how the Israelites failed to obtain the grace of God and so his righteousness.

4. To understand the vital importance of "preaching"—the presentation of the good news, the word of God, in God's plan of salvation.

5. To see how God, in fulfilling his covenants and promises, has made salvation available to all, both Jew and Gentile, on the same basis; thus, neither has any ground for boasting or feeling superior.

In this important section of Romans, Paul
returns to deal thoroughly with a question
which he has touched upon at various points in
the letter. (See especially Romans 2:12-3:31 in
Chapter 3 of this book.) The question may be
stated, Where do the literal Israelites or Jews
stand, in the light of God's new covenant
through Christ and the inclusion of all persons
in the offer of salvation by grace?

9:1-5

While Paul had felt strongly God's call to be
an "apostle to the Gentiles" and had answered
that call with his whole being, he still felt
keenly his kinship with other Jews and was
deeply concerned about their spiritual welfare.
The strength of this concern is indicated by his
words, "I could wish myself accursed from
Christ in behalf of my brothers, my relatives
according to the flesh" (9:3). This burden causes
him "great sorrow and unceasing anguish" in
his heart. These literal relatives of Paul have
had many advantages and many blessings from
God: They are Israelites and they possess the
sonship, the glory, the covenants, the law, the
system of worship or religious service, the
promises, the "fathers" (Abraham, Isaac, Jacob,
and the twelve tribal heads particularly), and
from them according to the flesh (according to
physical descent) came the Christ. Note carefully the words "according to the flesh" in this
passage and others; this term, referring here to

physical descent or lineage, is extremely significant in the development of Paul's thesis in this
section. He will shortly demonstrate that while
such descent is of some benefit, it does not
make one a part of God's new "elect" people.
Typically, as he thinks of God's multiplied blessings to his people, Paul injects a brief but fer-
vent expression of praise to God—"May God be
blessed forever. Amen!" (9:5).

9:6-29

Has God's word "failed," then, since literal
Israelite descent no longer qualifies one for
membership in God's elect, or for participation
in the fulfillment of the promise? No indeed,
answers Paul; God's intentions or promises
have not been defeated nor have they failed.
Rather, certain conditions have changed, conditions which have to do with people and their
standing in God's sight. These are set forth as
follows:

1. Not all those who are descended from
Israel are Israel. That is, not all who claim physical descent from Israel (Jacob) are part of God's
new Israel, his new "chosen people."

2. Not all those who are literal descendants
of Abraham are really children of Abraham, in
the most important sense.

3. God chose to name and continue Abraham's lineage through Isaac rather than Ish-
mael; and Isaac was a "child of promise," given
by faith rather than by human powers of

reproduction. Therefore, the criterion for participating in the promise of God becomes faith rather than works or "human lineage." This element of God's call or election, and faith as its response, continues in the cases of Jacob and Esau. The quotation from Malachi 1:2-3, "I loved Jacob, but I hated Esau," might better be translated, "I chose Jacob, but I rejected Esau." The Hebrew idiom involved in this statement indicates that God preferred the one over the other.

4. God's exercise of his prerogatives in electing (choosing) and rejecting does not indicate that he is unjust or capricious. Paul points out, through the examples of a molder and what is molded and the potter and the clay, that God in his sovereignty has the right to work with, in, and through people to accomplish his purposes. Under the new covenant, as Paul will affirm shortly, God has chosen to express his call and election *in Christ*.

5. God's call and election is now offered to Gentiles as well as Jews, and some of both groups will respond to form the "new Israel." It is significant that Paul, having already identified himself by birth with the literal Jews, now identifies himself spiritually with those who comprise the "new Israel"—"us whom he has called, not from the Jews only but also from the Gentiles" (9:24). Again turning to the Old Testament, the apostle drives home the point that

some who formerly were not considered God's people have now become his people, and that "only a remnant" of literal Israel will be saved. The Lord will "accomplish his word on the earth"—his word of righteousness and justice—without partiality for Jew or Gentile.

9:30—10:13

In this section, two kinds of righteousness appear in sharp contrast—human righteousness, based upon obedience to law; and God's kind of righteousness, based on faith. Paul first shows that the Gentiles, who did not "pursue" righteousness (that is, did not seek to attain it by deeds) attained it through faith. In contrast, the Jews, who did pursue righteousness (that is, sought to be justified with God by works of law) did not attain fulfillment of the law, and so did not attain the righteousness which they were seeking. Again expressing his deep concern for his fellow Jews, Paul declares his "heart's desire and prayer to God for them" (10:1) for their salvation.

The Jews have "stumbled over the stumblingstone"—Christ—and so have not attained to God's kind of righteousness. In seeking to establish their own righteousness, through works of law, they ignorantly rejected the righteousness which comes from God, based upon faith. This righteousness must come through Christ, who is "the end [finish, fulfillment] of the law," so that true righteousness (justification) might

71

come to "everyone who believes." In verses 5-10, Paul again turns to the Old Testament, apparently quoting from Leviticus 18:5 and paraphrasing Deuteronomy 30:12-14, to compare the "righteousness based on law" and that "based upon faith." Under the old covenant, persons who have done the righteousness (righteous requirements) of the law order their lives and find their relationship to God by this law. On the other hand, in Christ, righteousness (justification) with God does not rest upon desire or attempt to "ascend into heaven to bring Christ down" (that is, to hasten the Messiah's coming by perfect obedience to the law) or to "descend into the depths to bring Christ up from the dead" (that is, to bring about the resurrection and the promised conditions of the new age). The Messiah has already appeared, and the new age of the kingdom has already dawned! God's new message is "the word of faith, which we preach," declaring that justification comes through confession of Jesus as Lord and belief in him as the risen Savior. There is "no distinction," for the call to salvation goes out to all, and the experience of salvation belongs to everyone who "believes" and "calls upon the name of the Lord."

10:14-21

How does the call to salvation go out, so that people may respond in faith and be saved? Paul gives the answer in graphic and positive form:

> For people to call upon God for salvation,
>   they must believe in him;
> For people to believe in God, they must hear
>   about him.
> For people to hear about God, someone must
>   proclaim him to them.
> For people to proclaim effectively God's salva-
>   tion, they must be sent by him.

So then, "faith results from what is heard, and
what is heard comes through the spoken word
about Christ" (10:17). Paul goes on quickly to
acknowledge that even though this is God's
method for revealing his plan of salvation, not
all who hear will accept. Israel serves as a prime
example of this; though they heard and knew,
they did not respond to the call. Thus, God
characterized them as a "disobedient and resisting people." Furthermore, Paul affirms, unbe-
lieving Israelites would be "put to shame" by
believing Gentiles.

11:1-10

Does this mean, then, that Israel has totally
resisted God's call and so has been totally
rejected by him? Again Paul employs the
emphatic negative phrase, "Let it not be!" or
"Certainly not!" He reinforces this by pointing
out his own Hebrew ancestry. There are among
the Israelites "a remnant," some whom God
"foreknew." It is important to note that Paul
does not say "predestined," but "foreknew."
They are "elected" or "chosen," not by some

whimsical act of God, but by virtue of their faith response to the call of God. This remnant is "chosen by grace," through the unmerited favor of God in Christ; therefore, their relationship to God rests not upon "works" but upon faith. Thus, though all Israel sought righteousness, only a remnant found it. The rest were possessed by a "spirit of stupor"—lack of perception and failure to understand. Even their acts of worship became a "snare and a trap" to them (see Amos 4:4-5; 5:21-24), and they suffered bondage and oppression because they turned away from God.

11:11-24

In this portion of chapter 11, Paul summarizes through illustration and further explanation the relationship of Jews to Gentiles under the new covenant and their common relationship to God:

1. When Israel "trespassed," salvation was brought to the Gentiles. (Paul himself was the instrument of just such a development.) One result of this was "to make them [the Jews] jealous," so that they might also seek salvation through justification by faith.

2. Since the trespass of the Jews led to "riches" for the world, and their defection led to "riches" for the Gentiles, their "fullness" (inclusion in the covenant) will mean much more.

3. Though Paul is "apostle to the Gentiles," he is still greatly concerned about the Jews, and

he thus makes the most of his ministry, hoping to stir up the Jews to envy and so "save some of them." This is in accordance with his statement in 1 Corinthians 9:22, where he declares his intention to be "all things to all men, so that he might save some."

4. The metaphors of the "first-fruit" of the "dough" and the "whole lump," and the "root and the branches" are based upon Old Testament sacrificial practices. The "root" or "first-fruit"—the remnant, the believing Jews who accepted salvation by faith in Christ—would ordinarily be considered sufficient to make all Israel acceptable to God, since he had dealt with Israel as a "chosen nation." However, in relation to the new covenant and Christ, some of the branches were "broken off" (that is, they lost their status as part of God's people) by unbelief. In their place "wild olive branches"—the believing Gentiles who were not part of the original "stock" of God's elect people—were "grafted in."

5. These "wild olive branches" have no cause to boast or to feel superior to the original branches which were cut off. Paul admonishes them strongly: "So do not be conceited, but fear [stand in awe]" (11:20). *Faith or unbelief* is the key; the "natural branches" lost their place because of unbelief, and the "wild branches" were included because of faith. By the same token the "natural branches" can be restored through faith, and the "wild branches" can lose their relationship through apostasy or unbelief.

6. Again warning the Gentiles against being "wise in their own conceits," Paul explains for them a "mystery"; a "hardening" has come upon part of literal Israel, causing them to reject Christ and so be rejected by God. Furthermore, many of the Gentiles have come into right relationship with God through faith along with the believing "remnant" of Jews. These constitute the "new Israel," the *spiritual* Israel. Verse 26 sets forth the conclusion: "Thus [in this manner, in this way] all Israel shall be saved." Indeed, the "grace-gift and call of God are irrevocable" (11:29). God has not gone back on his promises or his covenant with Abraham or with Israel. All who respond in faith, both Jew and Gentile, are true descendants of Abraham and true Israelites, and thus "all [spiritual] Israel shall be saved" through the taking away of their sins (forgiveness) and faith. All persons, both Jew and Gentile, have been "shut up together" (placed in the same category) because of disobedience, and all must be saved through faith.

11:33-36

As Paul expounded upon God's plan for salvation, offered to everyone, he apparently was overwhelmed, as he often was in his spirit, by the greatness of God. On this occasion, he uttered one of the most profound and stirring doxologies in all the New Testament. The closing verse is especially inspiring: "For from him and through him and for him are all things. To

Him be glory forever! Amen."

Study and Review Questions for Chapter 8:

1. What was Paul's personal attitude and feeling concerning his fellow Jews and their relationship to God?

2. Who are the true (spiritual) descendants of Abraham and Jacob? How do they qualify for this relationship?

3. What kind of righteousness (justification) did the Jews seek? Why was this not pleasing to God?

4. How can a person find salvation and justification under the new covenant in Christ?

5. Explain Paul's statement in Romans 11:26, "And in this manner all Israel will be saved."

Chapter 9
A Living Sacrifice—
Members of the Body

Romans 12

Objectives for Chapter 9:

1. To learn what it means to "present your bodies a living sacrifice, holy and well-pleasing to God."

2. To discover how the church, or body of Christ, is like the human body, and what this signifies in terms of Christian relationships.

3. To learn how the "grace-gifts" are to be used or exercised in the church.

4. To develop Christian attitudes toward those who are hostile or evil.

The beginning of chapter 12 marks a major turning point in the Book of Romans. There is a definite connection in thought between the opening statement and what has gone before: *"Therefore,* I exhort you, brothers. . . ." But the focus shifts from the means of justification and Jewish-Gentile relationships to ethical demands of the gospel for all persons.

This general concern will be central in the remainder of the letter, until the final section of personal greetings and closing exhortations.

12:1, 2

In the first verses of this chapter, Paul challenges his readers to make a sacrifice of a higher and more personal kind than the animal sacrifices offered under the old covenant. "Therefore, I exhort you, brothers, through the mercies of God, to present your bodies a living sacrifice, holy and well-pleasing to God, your logical service." The phrase rendered here "logical service" is somewhat difficult to translate precisely into English and has been translated "reasonable service," "spiritual service," or "spiritual worship." In the Greek New Testament, the two terms signify that which is rational and logical of the inward mind or intent, and service or servitude, particularly religious service. As is implied by the translation "logical service," Paul seems to be referring to the inward acknowledgment of relationship which is owed to God and is appropriate from one who professes to be in right relationship to God. Verse 2 contains a negative command, and its corresponding affirmative: "Do not be conformed to this age, but be transformed by the renewing of the mind, that you may test what is the will of God, what is good and well-pleasing and complete." This passage is of vital significance to every Christian, and it is absolutely essential for spiritual growth. The Christian who wishes to reach spiritual maturity must be constantly seeking deeper understanding of God's will, and measuring every decision by the yardstick of "what is good, well-pleasing, and complete" (mature) in the Father's eyes.

12:3-8

Beginning another train of thought with a strong exhortation to humility, Paul supports the injunction by pointing out that the church of God is like the human body in its structural relationships. Each member of the body is important and has an important function to perform; and so no one member can claim superiority over another, since each is simply fulfilling its natural function in the body. So it is in the body of Christ: the members together comprise the whole body, but each member has a particular duty or duties to perform. In the church, these functions are not left to chance or mere human decision; each person is to perform the task "according to the measure of faith God has apportioned." Furthermore, as in the physical body, the members are interrelated; they depend upon and complement one another; or as Paul says, they are "individually members of one another" (12:5).

In most English versions, the term *charismata* is rendered "gifts." Actually, this term contains no form of the word for "gift" and means literally "things of grace" or "grace-things." Probably the best rendering is "grace-gifts," since they are things of God's grace or favor and are "given" by him for use in the body of Christ. Verses 6-8 then read, "Having grace-gifts which differ according to the grace which has been given to us, if prophecy, let it be according to the proportion of faith; if service, in serving; or he who teaches, in teaching; or he who exhorts, in exhortation; he who shares, in liberality; he who presides, with zeal; he who does acts of mercy, with cheerfulness."

This is one of the truly great passages in the New Testament regarding the grace-gifts and their use in the body of Christ. First, notice the various types of ministry or service which are required in the church: *Prophecy*—speaking forth for God, preaching. *Service*—this is the term *diakonia*, whose companion noun is *diakonos*, from which our English term *deacon* is derived by transliteration. It means "service," probably, in particular, caring for the material resources of the Christian body. The first "deacons" or servers in the church were those chosen by Jerusalem Christians to have charge of distributing necessities to the needy widows in the congregation. (See Acts 6:1-6.) *Teaching*—this was one of the most prominent and vital functions among the early Christians and ought to be so now. To become a teacher in the body involved great responsibility. James admonishes, "Let not many of you become teachers, my brothers, for we shall receive greater judgment" (James 3: 1). *Exhortation*—the term used here involves advocacy, encouragement, support. The "exhorter" can be a key person in strengthening others and in encouraging the body as a whole. *Sharing*—referring here primarily to actual giving or sharing of material means. *Presiding*—literally, "one who stands before" others; a leader, one in charge. Paul used this term on more than one occasion in referring to leaders of a local congregation; see, for example, 1 Thessalonians 5:12. *Doing acts of mercy*—this expression probably refers primarily to "alms-giving" or giving material gifts to the needy but would no doubt include more in the Christian community. A closely related word from the same root is employed to describe the good deeds which Dorcas had done for others before her death (Acts 9:36).

It is interesting to note the attitudes and spirit with which these grace-gifts are to be exercised in the body. Paul seems to be saying first to various ones who have these responsibilities, "Whatever your task is, get busy *doing* it! Then, he zeroes in on *how* and *in what spirit* this is to be done. Read the words again—"in liberality," "with zeal," "with cheerfulness." How do you give? How do you serve? How do you minister to others?

12:9-21

While the New Testament does not contain a

83

"book of law" like Leviticus or Deuteronomy, or a code like the Decalogue (Ten Commandments), it does give sound and definite rules of conduct for Christian living. This section of Romans 12 is of just such a nature. Touching first upon one of the fundamentals of Christian experience and life, the apostle enjoins, "Let love be without hypocrisy" (12:9). Even love can be faked! In the body of Christ, love must be sincere, genuine, from the heart. Furthermore, Christians are to "abhor the evil, (but) cling to the good." Examine yourself; do you really abhor the evil thing in what you say, what you read, what you think? And, just as vital, do you love and hold to what is good in all the same ways? Is your mind "set on things of the earth" or "set on things above?"

What about your relationship with others in the body; do you "love them with brotherly affection," and do you "take the lead in honoring" others? Even in the body of Christ, elements of jealousy, envy, or coldness can disrupt relationships and hinder the total witness. Attitudes of love, respect, and honor are meant to be mutual among God's people. *"Love one another* with brotherly affection," and "take the lead in giving honor to *one another."*

Endurance and enthusiasm are vital to the life and witness of the church. Every faithful worker in the body knows the importance of Paul's exhortation in these particular areas:

"Not letting up in zeal, glowing with the Spirit, doing service to the Lord" (12:11). When the work is difficult and the workers seem few, are you sometimes tempted to lose your enthusiasm? Do you live daily close to God, so that the glowing fire of the Spirit continually empowers you and inspires others through you? This kind of victory can belong constantly to you, if you are careful to remember that you are "serving God and not men." Verse 12 focuses upon four of the most important building blocks in developing Christian strength and maturity: "rejoicing," "hope," "patience" (endurance), and "prayer." As Paul often does, he exhorts the believers to be *rejoicing*—always. This is possible because of the Christian *hope,* hope which is eternal. In turn, because Christians have this eternal hope, they can endure even "tribulations" with *patience.* Christian patience is not an apathetic acceptance of "things as they are" or a fatalistic resignation. Rather, it is a patient endurance and determination, rooted in one's relationship to an eternal God and a living Lord. To sustain these qualities of joy, hope, and patience in all of life, the Christian is encouraged to "continue steadfastly in prayer." Through prayer faithful members of the body of Christ petition for others, give thanks, grow in spiritual maturity, and seek God's guidance.

Practically speaking, the Christian life is to be characterized by "sharing [literally, 'fellowshipping'] in the needs of the holy people, practicing hospitality" (12:13). While economic conditions and social circumstances have changed drastically since the first century, the need for these virtues is still very real. Modern Christians have more opportunities than ever to share in the needs of other Christians, at home and abroad. Are you taking advantage of some of these opportunities which are available to you and your congregation?

Verse 14 is strongly reminiscent of the teaching of Jesus, "Love your enemies, and pray for those who persecute you" (Matt. 5:44). Are you concerned, sympathetic, and empathetic with those who are experiencing sorrow, illness, or misfortune? Do you share with others the joy of a loved one saved, a body healed, a new baby, a special material blessing? Several admonitions on mutual relationships follow these exhortations—"Be in agreement with one another, not thinking exalted things [being haughty] but associating yourselves with the humble; do not become conceited" (12:16). Christians are further urged to live peaceably and to leave vengeance to God. As a member of the body, you are to be an agent of blessing rather than cursing, forgiveness rather than vengeance, harmony rather than dissension! Again we are reminded, at verse 20, of Jesus' own teaching: "If your enemy is hungry, feed him; if he is thirsty, give him a drink, for by so doing you will pile coals of fire upon his head." (That is, bring him under condemnation within himself and conviction, and hopefully to repentance.)

Summing up in principle these several verses regarding the Christian's response to enmity and evil, Paul says succinctly, "Do not be overcome by evil, but overcome evil with good." Doing evil, or returning evil for evil, is always a defeat for you as a Christian. Correspondingly, overcoming evil (persons or things) with good and right is always a victory—for you and for the cause of Christ!

Study and Review Questions for Chapter 9:

1. What does it mean to "present one's body as a living sacrifice?"

2. How does Paul compare the structure of the church with the human body in Romans 12?

3. What attitudes should prevail among Christians in using the grace-gifts in the church?

4. How should the Christian respond to enmity or persecution?

5. How can the Christian have victory over evil?

Chapter 10
Love, the Fulfilling
of the Law

Romans 13

Objectives for Chapter 10:

1. To learn how Christians should regard civil authorities, and why.

2. To learn what one thing Christians always owe to one another.

3. To understand how love is the fulfilling of the law.

4. To learn how Christians should conduct themselves until Christ returns.

13:1-7

In the first part of Romans 13, Paul speaks at some length to a question which was of immediate importance to the Christians of the first century, and it has continued to be so for the church in every century. That question is: What is—or ought to be—the attitude and relationship of Christian persons with reference to the political state (civil authority)? First a general principle is stated, clearly and unequivocally: "Let every person be in submission to the governing authorities" (13:1). This principle is given strong support in the verses which follow it; let us note carefully the logical sequence of development:

1. Every person is to be subject to the governing authorities.

2. Because God has instituted civil authority, it is his will that such authority continue to exist. Even among the Israelites, when there was no separation between religious and civil authorities and God ruled as king, principles and detailed laws were given for the ordering of human affairs. Paul does not say here and does not intend for his readers to believe that every individual civil official or every particular governmental system has God's approval and support. Obviously, this has not been so and will never be so. He does indicate that the *existence* and the *legitimate execution or exercise* of civil authority is willed by God for human society.

3. Therefore, since what we have just been discussing is true, "He who sets himself against the authority is resisting what God has appointed, and those who so position themselves will receive condemnation" (13:2). God has ordained that there should be legitimate authorities to order human affairs, and whoever opposes such authority is in effect opposing God himself. Again, it is important to notice that the word here does not indicate that any particular official or government is identifiable with God or with God's will. The principle of civil authority, and the exercise of that authority, is in harmony with God's will, and the Christian, as well as other persons, is to be subject to that authority. Rebellion against it is not pleasing to God and brings condemnation to those who practice it.

Verses 3 and 4 reveal what Paul considers to be the primary function (or one of the primary functions) of civil authority—to punish or suppress evil conduct and to encourage good conduct. "The rulers are not a terror [literally, a fear] to good conduct, but to evil." Persons, be they Christian or otherwise, who wish to be free from fear of civil authority must "do what is good"; thus they will not need to fear the authority but "will have approval from him." Drivers who exceed the speed limit or ignore traffic signals will be constantly looking over their shoulders, for they are violating the law, resisting the legitimate authority of government, and have reason for apprehension. On the other hand, those who drive lawfully and carefully can proceed in confidence and enjoy their drive, because they know they are not subject to arrest as lawbreakers. The authority is "the servant of God for your good"—that is, in the capacity as enforcer of law, the authority is carrying out a function which in principle is approved by God for the total general benefit of human society and the particular good of those who obey the law. By the same token, however, the wrongdoer has good reason to "be afraid," for the same authority who acts for the protection of those who do well also acts to inflict punishment and restraint upon the wrongdoer. As Paul says: "He does not carry the sword [symbol of punishment and authority] in vain."

Upon the basis of two good reasons, then, Christians are to be submissive to human authorities: to avoid punishment (actually, *God's* disapproval or wrath, since the human authority is carrying out what is ordered by God); and "on account of conscience." You may have a clear conscience toward God with regard to your service in the church, your giving, your personal morals; but what about the area of cooperation with and obedience to the laws and regulations of your employer, city, state, or nation? Many Christians violate their consciences by engaging in traffic violations; cheating on income tax returns; following dishonest (even if "approved") business practices; loafing on the job; violating office, shop, or factory regulations; or padding expense accounts!

Even the payment of taxes is based upon the principle of cooperation with civil authorities, for in this they are "servants of God attending to this very thing," just as those who punish wrongdoers. Thus, Christians are instructed to "pay to all what is due—taxes to whom taxes are due, revenue to whom revenue is due, respect [literally, 'fear'] to whom respect is due, honor to whom honor is due" (13:7). Often it may be that public officials (including tax-collectors!) are not themselves personally worthy of the respect of Christians or of any good citizen. Even in such cases, the Christian can and should respect the office held by such a person and the government which is represented. At the same time we remember that our allegiance in this area is not to any individual official or even to a particular system of government. Rather, it is ultimately to God, who has willed the existence and exercise of civil authority and who approves the legitimate operation of such authority.

13:8-10

Turning next to the concept of love, Paul again sounds a strong echo of the teaching of Jesus: "Owe no one anything except to love one another; for he who loves the other person has fulfilled [the] law" (13:8). Jesus, when asked about the greatest commandment, replied that it was total love toward God; then he added what Paul reiterates here: "And the second [greatest] is like it—you shall love your neighbor as yourself. On these two commandments depend all the law and the prophets." (See Matthew 22:37-40.) Paul states specifically that the commandments (that is the Decalogue in particular) and any other commandment are summed up in this statement, "You shall love your neighbor as yourself." How can this be so? Simply because the injunction to love involves far more than any specific or particular command or regulation. To love is to have "good will" toward another; that is, it involves not merely outward acts but also compassion and inner concern. "God so loved the world, that he gave. . . ." Love never works evil toward a neighbor, but good; and so it is the fulfillment of law. Love completes and carries out willingly and joyfully what law commands or demands, and more.

13:11-14

This section of Romans concludes with a stirring call for Christians to "be raised from sleep" (13:11). Paul reminds them that they know "the time, that it is already the hour for you to be raised from sleep." This indicates that "our salvation is nearer than when we believed." Paul is reminding the Christians of the fact that they are living in a new age, which will culminate in the resurrection and the final triumph of Christ and the forces of light. Their "salvation" will be made complete in the resurrection—they are already "saved," but the resurrection and then reunion with Christ will be the final act in the drama of God's "salvation history."

Continuing the imagery of "light" and "darkness" and focusing upon the urgency of the situation, Paul proclaims, "The night has passed on, the day has drawn near. So let us put away

94

the deeds of the darkness, and be clothed with the armor of light" (13:12). As modern Christians, knowing that many centuries have passed since these words were written, we may be tempted to attribute them to a mistaken theory of Paul that the parousia (return of Christ) was to come at any moment, and so feel that his writing here has little meaning for us. Such is by no means the case; on the contrary, these admonitions are as vital to Christians now as when they were written, and they possess a timeless significance. In every generation it is high time for Christians to be "raised from sleep" and to "put away the deeds of the darkness and be clothed in the armor of the light." The urgency of the gospel, of Christian vigilance, and of living in the light are ever upon us. The instructions given in verses 13 and 14, therefore, are not merely interim ethics, not given for a supposed brief time before a crisis. On the contrary, every generation calls for Christians who are willing to:

Conduct themselves becomingly, as in the day; not in revelings or drunkenness, not in sexual immorality and excesses, not in quarreling and jealousy; be clothed with the Lord Jesus Christ, and not make provision for the desires of the flesh.

The writer of 1 John says, "If we walk in the light, as he is in the light, we have fellowship with one another, and the blood of Jesus his

Son cleanses us from all sin" (1 John 1:7). If we have received the light of Christ within our hearts, let us conduct ourselves as "children of light," "put away the deeds of the darkness," and "be clothed with the Lord Jesus Christ!"

Study and Review Questions for Chapter 10:

1. What should be the Christian's attitude toward civil authorities?

2. What are some of the purposes for the existence of civil authorities?

3. What is the one thing for which Christians are always "indebted" to one another?

4. Explain the statement, "Love is the fulfillment of law."

5. How are Christians to conduct themselves as they anticipate the return of Christ?

Chapter 11
The Weak and the Strong

Romans 14:1-15:6

Objectives for Chapter 11:

1. To understand that there are both the "weak" and the "strong" in the church.

2. To learn how the "weak" and the "strong" should conduct themselves toward one another.

3. To discover the true meaning of being in the "kingdom of God," and what the kingdom is.

4. To learn how to deal with questions of conscience or individual opinion in the church.

14:1-9

Ever since the beginning of the church, there have been persons of varying degrees of maturity and understanding in the Christian fellowship. This is still as true as when Romans was written, but it is often given little or no consideration among the members of the body. Paul refers to the "weak" and the "strong" among the Christians and gives inspired and inspiring guidance regarding their relationship in the church.

The first principle with reference to one who is "weak in the faith" is an important one: "Take to yourselves the one who is weak in the faith, [but] not for disputes over opinions." This does not regard spiritual matters or basic doctrines of Christ or the church. Rather, it concerns "opinions" or "matters of discussion," of which Paul gives an immediate example—scruples or regulations concerning the eating of certain foods. In many cases, probably, both Old Testament and Hellenistic elements were involved in such questions among the Roman Christians. While one person has faith to eat all kinds of food, another, who is "weak," eats only vegetables. How shall these two, with differing opinions or practices at this particular point, live and work in harmony in the church? The responsibility is mutual: "Let the one who eats not have contempt toward the one who does not eat," and on the other hand, "Let the one who does not eat not condemn the one who eats, for God has accepted him" (14:3). Those who condemn or criticize another in such circumstances find themselves guilty of "judging the household servant of another." This is not acceptable or valid, since all servants "stand or fall" before their own master; they are not required to answer to another. Furthermore, in the case of a Christian, Paul hastens to add, "he will be made to stand, for the Master [whom he serves, that is, Christ the Lord] is able to make him stand." If God has accepted the "weak" one, others of the fellowship—even the "strong"—must also accept and help that one to become one of the "strong!"

Another area in which differences of opinion often arose was in the observance of certain days as "special" or "holy" days. Again, it is likely that such issues arose from both Jewish and non-Jewish backgrounds and practices. Whatever each person practices, says Paul, "let each be fully assured in his own mind" (14:5). That is, let all persons be sure that their practice is based on worthy and sincere motives and that they observe, eat, or abstain "to the Lord." In this way, each can honor God, do service to him and "give thanks to God." Everything which believers observe, practice, and do—even their very lives and deaths—ought to be done "to the Lord" and not to themselves. The most elaborate rituals, the most rigid observances, the most stringent disciplines are in vain if done for selfish purposes or with unworthy motives. Correspondingly, God honors what is done "to the Lord" from a thankful and trusting heart. Stating a cardinal principle of his own service to God, Paul affirms the ultimate commitment and destiny of the faithful Christian: "If we live we live to the Lord, and if we die we die to the Lord; so then, whether we live or whether we die, we belong to the Lord" (14:8). Indeed, this was the purpose of Christ's own death and ris-

ing to new life, "so that he might be Lord of both the dead and the living."
14:10-13

The principle of common responsibility to God and mutual responsibility to each other is brought into sharp focus in this section. Paul confronts his readers directly and reminds them that they all alike must answer to God and be finally judged by him: "Now you, why do you condemn your brother? Or you, why do you have contempt for your brother? for we shall all stand before the judgment seat of God." As he often does, the apostle reinforces this affirmation by a quotation from the Old Testament, this time from Isaiah 45:23. Since all persons are liable to the judgment of God, it behooves all to refrain from passing judgment on one another. Furthermore, simply to refrain from judging or condemning another is not sufficient. Each person should determine "not to place a hindrance or stumbling block before a brother" (14:13). At this point, the concept of the "weak" and the "strong" enters again into Paul's thought, along with consideration of the individual conscience.

Paul knows, as most modern Christians know, that "nothing is unclean [literally, common] of itself." At the same time, he also recognizes that "it is unclean for anyone who thinks it to be unclean." If, therefore, a "strong" brother or sister, acting only according to personal desires and understanding, offends or injures the conscience and experience of a "weak" person, then he or she is "not walking according to love." What a shame it would be to "destroy by your food one for whom Christ died." Yet this very thing can happen when Christians ignore the principle of mutual concern and consideration. For "strong" Christians, their boldness and freedom from binding regulations or scruples may indeed be "good" and intended for good. Paul recognizes this fact, classifying himself among the "strong"; yet at the same time he warns against selfish and inconsiderate exercise of such freedom. If another believer is harmed by it, then the "strong" believer's "good" will be "blasphemed," spoken of as evil.

All this is based upon a fundamental truth about the nature of the kingdom (reign) of God and about the essence of Christian service. "The kingdom of God is not food and drink, but righteousness and peace and joy in the Holy Spirit. The one who serves the Christ in this manner is well-pleasing to God and approved to men" (14:17-18). The rule of God in one's life, then, is not predicated upon outward observances or rituals of any kind, but upon the state of the "inner man." *Righteousness* is present because the person has been justified through the blood of Christ. *Peace* is present because Christ has given a peace within the heart which the world cannot give, peace with God and others. *Joy* is present because the believer can re-joice whatever comes, knowing that victory is complete and hope is eternal. All of these are possessed and enjoyed "in the Holy Spirit" as the Spirit teaches, guides, and inspires all of life.

In view of this, then, Paul urges: "Let us pursue the things of peace and the things of building up one another" (14:19). Harmony and mutual edification result when believers, both "weak" and "strong," aim at peaceful and helpful relationships in questions of conscience as well as other matters. Drawing from his own en-lightenment and understanding, Paul affirms, "In fact, all things are clean." Nevertheless, a thing can become evil or bad for one to whom eating it is a stumbling block or cause for sin. Therefore, "it is good not to eat meat or drink wine or do anything by which your brother stumbles." As a Christian, are you willing to give first consideration to "weak" ones and their conscience and growth, putting your own per-sonal desires or feelings in second place? Have you known of specific cases in which a "weak" Christian has been harmed, offended, or dis-couraged by lack of consideration on the part of stronger, more mature Christians?

In addition to giving due consideration to others in the body in the way in which one lives, one must also maintain a clear conscience with God and within one's own mind and heart. Are you truly at ease within yourself, in God's sight, about what you do (or abstain from doing); or are you acting from outside pressures or opinions? Paul admonishes, "The faith which you have regarding yourself, have it before God. Happy is he who does not condemn himself in what he approves. But he who doubts has been condemned if he eats, because it is not from faith. Everything which is not from faith is sin" (14:22-23). Whatever the opinion, practice, or conviction of others might be, each person ultimately answers to God individually. It is far better to be "over-scrupulous" in a given matter than to proceed with doubt or lack of faith and sin against one's self and so against God.

15:1-6

Summing up his discussion of the "weak" and the "strong" and their relationships in the church, Paul employs the first person plural, thus making the appeal very personal. First, he points out that "we who are strong" have an obligation to "bear the weaknesses of those who are not strong." New Christians, in particular, often need this kind of help and support. How can they grow stronger and reach maturity in the faith without the help and consideration of their brothers and sisters in the fellowship? Furthermore, a broader obligation touches each member of the body. Rather than "pleasing ourselves," let each person "please his neighbor for good, toward edification." The example of Christ comes forward at this point.

Here is one who "did not please himself," but bore the reproaches and sins of God's enemies upon himself. Having just quoted from Psalm 69:9 in 15:3, Paul reminds his readers that the sacred writings had been produced for their learning at a later time. Through them, Christians can find "steadfastness," "encouragement," and "hope." In a typical expression of enthusiasm and benediction, the apostle wishes for them harmony and accord with Christ Jesus, from "the God of steadfastness and encouragement," to the end that they may "with one voice glorify the God and Father of our Lord Jesus Christ." Certainly, Christians who live together in a spirit of mutual helpfulness, consideration, and support can glorify God—both within the fellowship and in the eyes of those outside.

Study and Review Questions for Chapter 11:

1. How should persons who are "weak in the faith" (including new Christians) be regarded by other Christians?

2. Why does one Christian not have a right to pass judgment on or condemn another?

3. What are some questions of conscience or individual opinion which must be faced and dealt with in modern Christian life?

4. What really constitutes experience and life in the kingdom of God (under God's reign)?

5. How should the "weak" and the "strong" in the church regard and treat one another?

Chapter 12
The Gentiles, an Offering for God

Romans 15:7-33

Objectives for Chapter 12:

1. To see Christ as an example for Christians in their mutual relationships.

2. To grasp what Paul's ministry and call meant to him as "apostle to the Gentiles."

3. To understand Paul's reasons for wanting to visit the Roman Christians and his further plans for spreading the good news.

Continuing in the same general area of concern but focusing upon a somewhat different aspect, Paul begins to speak of how the Gentiles (literally, the nations) have been accepted by God, through Christ, and how this serves as an example for the Christians' acceptance of one another. This will lead, later in the chapter, to a restatement of Paul's commission as "apostle to the Gentiles."

15:7-12

The Christians are to "accept one another" as

Christ accepted them, "to the glory of God." Christ became a "servant of circumcision" (that is, submitted himself to the ordinances of Judaism, was born—humanly speaking—of the Jews, and proclaimed the good news of the Kingdom first to the Jews). He did this so that the promises of God to the patriarchs and to Israel might be fulfilled, and so that, as the good news was extended to all persons through Christ, the Gentiles might "glorify God because of [his] mercies" (15:9). This was the plan and will of God from of old, as Paul shows by quotations (in vv. 10, 11, 12, respectively) from Deuteronomy 32:43, Psalm 117, and Isaiah 11:10. The Gentiles were to become a part of "his people," to proclaim praise to God, to accept Christ as spiritual ruler or king, and to find an eternal "hope" in him. All of these have been fulfilled in and through Christ as the good news of his salvation has been proclaimed to the non-Jews. Thus through Christ and in part through Paul's own ministry, God has brought to fruition the promises or covenants which he made with Israel as his people and has also extended the opportunity for salvation to the Gentiles. In this way, all who believe are made acceptable to Christ, both Jew and Gentile, and so they are obligated to accept one another in the Christian fellowship.

15:13-22

Turning again to the actual experience and

condition of his readers, Paul expresses his prayer that the "God of hope" would fill them with "joy and peace" as they believe in him. If God is allowed so to work in and fill them, Paul is confident that they will, as a result, "abound in hope by the power of the Holy Spirit" (15:13). Lest his readers think that he does not give proper credence to their present experience and maturity, and perhaps in preparation for the appeal which he will shortly make to them, the apostle next mentions his confidence that they are "full of goodness, having been filled with all knowledge, and able to admonish one another." Nevertheless, he has seen fit to write them concerning certain matters as an additional reminder. This action has been taken on the basis of the "grace" which was given to Paul as a "special servant of Christ Jesus to the Gentiles," ministering the "good news of God" to them. While Paul was deeply concerned about his fellow Jews, and exerted strenuous effort toward their salvation, he felt keenly his call from God to be "apostle to the Gentiles." Two terms in verse 16 of this section give significant insight into this concept of a special ministry, as Paul viewed it. The first, rendered as *special servant*, is the basis of our English term *liturgy* and refers to specific religious service, particularly in a sanctuary of worship. The second has as its root the Greek term signifying a *priest*, and may be translated "priestly service" or "sacred service." Thus, Paul sees his ministry as one of a "special servant of Christ Jesus to the Gentiles, ministering the good news of God to them as a priest." For this call and ministry Paul gave up everything, including his very life, and pursued it to the end with joy and victory. How seriously do you take the call of God upon your life? If you have been called to special service in the work of God and the church, how have you responded to that call? Are you willing to respond affirmatively should such a call come?

This ministry, of course, had a purpose: "So that the offering of the Gentiles might be acceptable, having been sanctified [made holy] by the Holy Spirit" (15:16). Formerly, the Gentiles were not "acceptable"; with the coming of Christ and the new covenant, they can become acceptable to God, along with the Jews. Both, however, must be "made holy by the Holy Spirit." To this end, particularly regarding the Gentiles, Paul preached, worked, and lived.

Paul was always careful, as any Christian leader or worker should be, to avoid the impression that he was proud of his work for God, in a selfish sense, or that he was "humanly boasting" about the accomplishments of his ministry to the Gentiles. Here, having spoken rather boldly of that ministry, he hastens to say that he has reasons for boasting about what God has done—but only "in Christ." Thus, he does not presume to speak of anything except "what Christ has accomplished through me for the obedience of the Gentiles" (15:18). In accomplishing these things through Paul, Christ worked by means of word and deed, by the power of signs and wonders, by the power of the Spirit. The Acts account of Paul's ministry, and his own statements at several points in his letters, bear ample testimony that Christ indeed worked in all these ways through Paul. As a result, Paul had fulfilled his commission to proclaim the good news "from Jerusalem, and round about as far as Illyricum." The New Testament contains no specific reference to Paul's working in Illyricum, an area lying between the Adriatic Sea and the Danube River (today, Albania). Nevertheless, "from Macedonia the *Via Egnatia* struck across the Balkans to the eastern coast of the Adriatic, and it is not impossible that Paul or his associates had made tentative excursions in this direction as far as Illyricum."* As ambassador for Christ, Paul has "made it an ambition" to evangelize in new areas "where Christ was not named," that is, known and acknowledged as Lord and Savior. The great apostle did not wish to "build upon the foundations of another" but rather to fulfill the prophecy of Isaiah 52:15 which declares: "Those who have not been told about him shall see, and those who have not heard will understand." This desire to reach untouched areas for Christ had, in fact, prevented Paul "many times" from coming to see the Roman Christians face-to-face. But now a different prospect appears, as he is about to make known to them.

15:23-33

Since Paul "no longer has room" for work (his particular type of work) in the area where he finds himself, he feels that now is an opportune time to carry out his long held desire to visit the Christians at Rome. This visit, however, was not the end goal of his proposed journey into that part of the world. As always, the call of God to be "apostle to the Gentiles" was uppermost in Paul's mind and purpose. He hoped to see the Roman believers only as he was "passing through" on his way to Spain; he planned to have the pleasure of their company "for a short time" (15:23-24). In addition, he hoped "to be sped on his journey there" by the Roman Christians. The term used here is literally "to be sent forward." Certainly Paul hoped to have the encouragement and good wishes of the Roman Christians. However, he may have had in mind also appealing to them for material assistance and backing for his missionary enterprise in Spain.

Before Paul could embark on the long-awaited journey to Spain via Rome, he had another task to accomplish—the deliverance of the aid sent from Christians in other areas to the needy Christians in Jerusalem and Judea. (See Acts 20 and 21 for other references to this journey, its results, and the practice of sending contributions from one group of Christians to another.) Christians of "Macedonia and Achaia" (Greece) are specifically named here as contributing to a relief fund for the Judean believers. Paul injects at this point his personal feeling that this was only right. Since the Gentiles had shared in the "spiritual things" of the Jewish Christians, they should be willing to be of service to them in turn in "fleshly [material] things" (15:27). Having completed this important task, Paul plans to go on to Spain, visiting the Roman Christians on the way. Perhaps to further prepare the way for himself and encourage them to assist him, the apostle adds, "and I know that when I come to you, I will come in the fullness of the blessing of Christ."

In verses 30 and 31, Paul reveals a grave concern regarding his planned trip to Jerusalem. We know from his remarks to the leaders of the church at Ephesus that he did expect serious difficulties at Jerusalem, and he was uncertain about the outcome of his journey there. (See Acts 20:22-23.) Often we find Paul requesting the interest and prayers of his readers; this appeal, however, is particularly urgent and emphatic: "I appeal to you, brothers, through our Lord Jesus Christ and through the love of the Spirit, to agonize with me in prayers to God in my behalf, that I may be delivered from the disobedient in Judea, and that my service for Jerusalem will be well-pleasing to the holy people, so that I may come to you in joy by the will of God, to be refreshed by you." Even in such an urgent personal appeal, the apostle is most deeply concerned about the success of his work for the Lord rather than about his personal safety. His wish for rescue from "the disobedient in Judea" is prompted by his intense desire and ambition to complete the intended service to the Jerusalem Christians and then to go on to Rome as one more step in the journey to new fields of labor in Spain. As usual, Paul closes this section of exhortation and appeal with a thought in behalf of his readers: "May the God of peace be with all of you. Amen."

Study and Review Questions for Chapter 12:

1. How does Christ serve as an example to Christians in their acceptance of one another?

2. Upon what basis did Paul feel that he had a right to instruct, remind, and exhort the Roman Christians?

3. Through what specific ways did God work through Paul? Does he work in all of these ways today?

4. What were the apparent or probable reasons for Paul's desire to visit the Roman Christians?

5. How did Paul request the Roman Christians to pray for him?

---

*C. K. Banett, *The Epistle to the Romans* (New York: Harper & Row. 1957), p. 276.

Chapter 13
Name Them One by One

Romans 16

Objectives for Chapter 13:

1. To see that many of the persons named in Romans 16 are familiar from other New Testament references, and note how they played a part in Paul's ministry and experience.

2. To realize the warm and profound relationships which Paul developed with those who worked with him in the labor of the Lord.

3. To learn how Christians can deal with persons who cause problems in the church.

4. To experience and thrill to the impact of the inspired doxology which closes the letter to the Romans.

5. To review the key teachings and themes of Romans.

This final section of Romans consists largely of personal greetings and references. It reveals that Paul was acquainted with a number of individuals who were a part of the congregation at Rome, some of whom are familiar to us from other New Testament references. The greetings include both those from Paul to persons at Rome, and those from Paul's companions to the Roman Christians.

16:1-2

The first person to come under consideration is one Phoebe, who is described as "our sister" and "a server [deacon] of the church at Cenchreae." Paul commends this woman to the Roman Christians, urging them to accept her "in the Lord, in a manner worthy of the holy people," and to help her in whatever she may need, for she has been "a supporter of many and of me myself." The term here translated *supporter* signifies one who furthers the work of another or the interests of another. Phoebe may have given support to Paul and other Christians by her work, through financial and material support, or in other ways.

16:3-16

Some twenty-six persons are named in this section, and they represent a considerably greater number, since Paul in some instances refers to "the family" of a certain individual or to "the brothers [or the holy people] who are with them" (16:14). Some of the individuals named have particular interest to us because of other references to them or because of what is indicated concerning them. This is true of "Prisca [shortened form of Priscilla] and Aquila, my fellow workers in Christ Jesus, who risked their necks for my life." This couple is known to us from Acts 18 and is referred to in 1 Corinthians 16:19. Paul had met them in Corinth, where they had moved when Claudius ordered all the Jews to leave Rome (A.D. 49). We do not know of the specific instance when they "risked their necks" for Paul. Greetings are sent also to "the church in their house."

Special greeting is given to Epaenetus, apparently the first convert which Paul made for Christ in Asia. Andronicus and Junias are called Paul's "kinsmen" (apparently meaning fellow Jews) and "fellow prisoners" and are said to have been "in Christ" (saved) before the apostle himself.

The "Rufus" mentioned in verse 13 is thought by many commentators to be the Rufus mentioned in Mark 15:21 as one of the sons of Simon of Cyrene. Paul evidently felt warm relationship with this man and his family, for he refers to Rufus as "the chosen one in the Lord" and sends greetings to "his mother, [who is] also mine."

Bringing to a close his own personal greetings to men and women in the Roman church, Paul admonishes them to "greet one another with a holy kiss" (16:16), and adds "all the churches of Christ greet you." This last salutation apparently was meant to represent the congregations in the area from which Paul was writing and working, or, perhaps even more extensively, all the congregations in the eastern

Mediterranean area, as Paul prepared to go
west to Rome and Spain with the good news.

16:17-20

Before turning to greetings sent by his companions to the Roman church, Paul pauses to
warn against dissension and deception in the
church. Given his obvious personal knowledge
of many individuals in the congregation at
Rome, the apostle may well have known of particular problems which existed there in these
areas. At any rate, he cautions them to "take
note" of persons who cause dissensions and difficulties (stumbling blocks) contrary to the
teachings which they had learned. The Roman
Christians are urged to "keep away from them,"
for such persons are not sincerely serving the
Lord. Rather, they "serve their own belly"
(probably a reference to a preoccupation among
Jewish believers with food or dietary laws and
regulations, rather than gluttony) and by
deceiving speech lead astray "the hearts of the
innocent" (credulous).

Paul has confidence in the sincerity and "obedience" of the Roman Christians, but still he
feels it necessary to warn them against deception and guile. Again using the expression "the
God of peace," the apostle assures his readers
that this God will "crush Satan under your feet
swiftly" (16:20). Certainly it was encouraging to
the Christians at Rome and is just as encouraging to Christians today, to know that they are

not alone in their battle against sin, deception, legalism, and division. God is with those who love and obey him; he gives them victory daily in this life and this age and will give them eternal victory when the prince of evil is "crushed" for the last time and the new age begins!

16:21-23

After invoking "the grace of our Lord Jesus Christ" (16:20) once more upon his readers, Paul expresses personal greetings from some who were with him as he wrote. Again, some familiar names appear: Timothy, a companion of Paul in much of his work and a leader in the church; Jason (Acts 17:5-9); Sosipater (Acts 20:4, where the form "Sopater" is found, probably referring to the same person). Tertius, "the one who has written the letter," sends personal greetings "in the Lord." Apparently this man was both an able scribe and a Christian. (It is probable that Paul often, perhaps always, dictated his letters. See, for example, 1 Corinthians 16:21, Galatians 6:11, Colossians 4:18, 2 Thessalonians 3:17.) Gaius may well be the same person by that name who appears in Acts 19:29 and 20:4; 1 Corinthians 1:14; and 3 John 1. Erastus was a fellow worker of Paul's along with Timothy and is mentioned in Acts 19:22 and 2 Timothy 4:20. Here in Romans, he appears to be a city official, a "steward of the city."

One of the most inspiring and complete doxologies (glorifications of God) in the Pauline
writings brings to a close the great letter to the
Roman church. Notice Paul's exalted description
of God, with reference to his worthiness to
receive glory, praise, and honor:

Him who is able to establish you;
He has kept "the mystery" (the good news of
    salvation through Christ) secret for "long
    ages"
But now has "revealed it through the pro-
    phetic writings" to all nations;
He is "the eternal God," the "only wise God,"
    and so "to him be glory forever through
    Jesus Christ! Amen."

A fitting finish indeed for such an immortal
writing! For the glory of God Paul lived,
worked, preached, endured, and wrote; for the
glory of God he went to prison, and for the
glory of God he died. May God grant that you
will be inspired to follow in the apostle's foot-
steps, and therefore those of his Master,
through this inspired masterpiece of the Letter
to the Romans.

Study and Review Questions for Chapter 13:

1. Which of the persons named in Romans
16 are known from other New Testament references? What do we know about them?

2. How should Christians deal with persons

who cause divisions, offenses, and deception in the church?

3. What does it mean to be "wise as to what is good, but guileless as to what is evil" (Romans 16:19)?

4. Why did Tertius describe himself as "the one having written the letter?"

5. Find other doxologies similar to Romans 16:25-27, both in Paul's letters and in other New Testament writings.

Major Themes and Teachings of Romans:

Now that you have completed a detailed study of the Letter to the Romans, what are the ideas, revelations, and facts which have been most helpful, enlightening, or inspirational to you? Here are some major categories of thought or subject matter to help start you on this quest:

1. The position or situation of persons who know of God, or have opportunity to know of him, but do not acknowledge or serve him.

2. The relationship of the "new Israel" or the church, the body of Christ, to the literal Jews, under Christ.

3. The fulfillment of God's covenant with Abraham and Israel, in terms of the Christian gospel and salvation offered to all persons.

4. The meaning of being "justified" (made righteous by faith, as opposed to being "justified by works of law").

5. The relationship of Christians to sin and

its power; the results of sin and righteousness, respectively.

6. The role of the Spirit in Christian victory and life.

7. The relationships of Christians to one another and to the world as members of the body of Christ.

8. How the whole requirement of law is fulfilled by love.

9. The identity of the "weak" and the "strong" in the church, and their mutual relationships.

10. How Christians can deal individually and/or collectively with division or dissension in the church.